# Victorian Poetry

## Blackwell Essential Literature

# Victorian Poetry

*Edited by* Duncan Wu

based on
*The Victorians:*
*An Anthology of Poetry and Poetics*

*edited by* Valentine Cunningham

**Blackwell**
Publishing

Editorial Offices:
108 Cowley Road, Oxford OX4 1JF, UK
Tel: +44 (0) 1865 791100
350 Main Street,
Malden, MA 02148-5018, USA
Tel: +1 781 388 8250

First published 2002 by Blackwell Publishers Ltd.

Library of Congress Cataloging-in-Publication Data

Victorian poetry / edited by Duncan Wu.
p. cm. — (Blackwell essential literature)
"Based on The Victorians: an anthology of poetry and poetics,
edited by Valentine Cunningham."
Includes bibliographical references and index.
ISBN 0-631-23075-0 (alk. paper)—ISBN 0-631-23076-9 (pbk. : alk. paper)
1. English poetry—19th century. I. Wu, Duncan. II. Victorians. III. Series.
PR1223 .V53 2002      821'.808—dc21      2002020878

A catalogue record for this title is available from the British Library

Set in 8/10pt Galliard
by Kolam Information Services Pvt. Ltd, Pondicherry, India
Printed and bound at T.J. International Ltd, Padstow, Cornwall

For further information on
Blackwell Publishers, visit our website:
www.blackwellpublishers.com

# Contents

## Emily (Jane) Brontë (1818–1848)

## Arthur Hugh Clough (1819–1861)

## Matthew Arnold (1822–1888)

## Dante Gabriel Rossetti (1828–1882)

## Christina G. Rossetti (1830–1894)

## Thomas Hardy (1840–1928)

## Gerard Manley Hopkins (1844–1889)

# A. E. Housman (1859–1936)

# William Butler Yeats (1865–1939)

# Index of Titles and First Lines

# Series Editor's Preface

The Blackwell Essential Literature series offers readers the chance to possess authoritative texts of key poems (and in one case drama) across the standard periods and movements. Based on correspondent volumes in the Blackwell Anthologies series, most of these volumes run to no more than 200 pages. The acknowledged virtues of the Blackwell Anthologies are range and variety; those of the Essential Literature series are authoritative selection, compactness and ease of use. They will be particularly helpful to students hard-pressed for time, who need a digest of the poetry of each historical period.

In selecting the contents of each volume particular attention has been given to major writers whose works are widely taught at most schools and universities. Each volume contains a general introduction designed to introduce the reader to those central works.

Together, these volumes comprise a crucial resource for anyone who reads or studies poetry.

Duncan Wu
St Catherine's College, Oxford

# Introduction

## Duncan Wu

Recent anthologies of Victorian poetry and prose have provided readers with a remarkably diverse and wide-ranging body of work. Valentine Cunningham's invaluable *The Victorians* ranges from the late works of Wordsworth and Leigh Hunt at one end of the century to Yeats, Housman and Kipling at the other. In between he offers a rich selection of verse, including anonymous street ballads; the poetry of women poets such as Caroline Norton, Fanny Kemble, Jemima Luke, Eliza Cook and Dora Greenwell; as well as rural writers like John Clare, Ebenezer Elliot and William Barnes. The diversity is highlighted by Professor Cunningham in his introduction:

> So here are poems about cod-liver oil, railway lines and railway trains, chairs, soup, soap, paintings, omnibuses, going to the dentist, Grimm's Law, weather in the suburbs, dead dogs, cricket players, a cabbage leaf, Missing Links, tobacco, booze, snow, sado-masochism, Psychical Research, leeks, onions, genitalia, war, New Women, fairies, love, death, God, pain, poverty, poems, faith, doubt, science, poets, poetry.[1]

For range readers will require *The Victorians* – and, should they desire even more, other anthologies of Victorian writing, which reflect the catholicity of interest within the period. This volume aims to do something different. It distills into a smaller space some of the most influential poetry of the period by Elizabeth Barrett Browning, Alfred (Lord) Tennyson, Robert Browning, Emily (Jane) Brontë, Arthur Hugh Clough, Matthew Arnold, Dante Gabriel Rossetti, Christina G. Rossetti, Thomas Hardy, Gerard Manley Hopkins, A. E. Housman and William Butler Yeats. Pressure of space necessarily denies admission to many of those anthologized by Professor Cunningham – James Thomson, George Meredith, William Morris, Lewis Carroll, W. E. Henley, Robert Louis Stevenson, to name a few.

What this selection lacks in range it makes up for in depth, including complete texts of 'Fra Lippo Lippi', 'The Prisoner', 'Dover Beach', 'The Scholar-Gipsy', 'The Blessed Damozel', 'Goblin Market' and 'The Wreck of the Deutschland'. The implied claim is not that these are representative – it would be virtually impossible to construct such a selection within a mere 180-odd pages – but that they are essential reading for anyone with an interest in verse of the period.

Tennyson and Browning predominate, as they are the major poets of the age. No less than the queen remarked to Tennyson that, 'Next to the Bible, *In Memoriam* is my comfort'. There are few better examples of the Victorian preoccupation with death and its aftermath. It is on the one hand an intensely private poem about one man's

---

[1] Valentine Cunningham, introduction, *The Victorians: An Anthology* (Oxford: Blackwell, 2000), p. xxxv.

grief for another, and on the other a work that speaks of the innermost anxieties of the age, exemplifying Auden's contention that Tennyson's gift was for expressing feelings of 'lonely terror and desire for death'.[2] The fruit of nearly 17 years' labour, it doubtless has its faults – it is relentless in its subjectivity, almost oppressively so – but it transcends the personal in addressing the anxieties arising from the nineteenth-century confrontation with evolutionary theories Tennyson had encountered in Robert Chambers's *Vestiges of Creation* and Charles Lyell's *Principles of Geology*.[3] The natural world of *In Memoriam* is not invariably, therefore, the divinely appointed one of Wordsworth; it can be, rather, 'red in tooth and claw',[4] the product of a cosmos lacking a benevolent deity. In this sense *In Memoriam*, the most successful long poem of its day, is a product of the *zeitgeist*, a growing scepticism that was to find fuller expression in the poetry of Hardy and Housman later in the century.

Tennyson's preoccupation with states of mind looks back to Wordsworth, and is found in shorter poems such as 'Tears, idle tears', which concerns the uncontrollable emotions that run deeply in the human heart. In such sonnets as 'Surprised by joy' Wordsworth had attempted the same kind of investigation.[5] For his part, Wordsworth possessed a copy of Tennyson's important 1842 *Poems*, and welcomed an acquaintance with their author.[6] By the time Wordsworth died in 1850 Tennyson was in his early forties and Browning in his late thirties. The influence of the Romantics was felt throughout the century, but their reign had ended: Tennyson and Browning were remaking the art.

Browning's major contribution, in common with that of Tennyson, was to develop a new kind of psychological poetry – one that explored the human mind from within, through the dramatic monologue. There were precedents in the Romantic period – all 'big six' poets had tried their hand at writing plays – but the achievement of Browning and Tennyson was to adapt the form so as to bring the science of disclosure through verbal nuance to a fine art. The Ulysses who in Tennyson's poem declares his desire 'To strive, to seek, to find, and not to yield' may not be the sort of sea-captain with whom we should set sail; from the very moment that the speaker of Browning's 'My Last Duchess' notes that the portrait of his former wife looks 'as if she were alive' we know that this is no mere compliment to the painter, Frà Pandolf – there is something darker at work. And when the speaker of 'A Toccata of Galuppi's' tells us that he feels 'chilly and grown old', something rather important has happened, on a level beyond the verbal, which it is for us to infer. As readers of such poetry we are in a privileged position; Tennyson and Browning exploited the form aware that our knowing so much more than their speakers, comprehending moral failings with a clarity not always vouchsafed in life, was the key to a new poetic. Its potential would be further championed in the modern period by Eliot and Pound.[7]

---

[2]  W. H. Auden, *Forewords and Afterwords* ed. Edward Mendelson (London: Faber, 1973), p. 226. E. Warwick Slinn helpfully contextualizes *In Memoriam* in his essay on Victorian poetry in *A Companion to Victorian Literature and Culture* ed. Herbert Tucker (Oxford: Blackwell, 1999), pp. 311–13.

[3]  See in particular *In Memoriam* lv and lvi.

[4]  *In Memoriam* lvi 15.

[5]  *The Prelude*, Wordsworth's most extensive examination of psychological process, was not published until 1850, the same year as *In Memoriam*.

[6]  See Robert Bernard Martin, *Tennyson: The Unquiet Heart* (London: Faber, 1983), pp. 289–91.

[7]  See for instance Pound's 'Piere Vidal Old' and Eliot's 'Prufrock', besides much else.

Browning's wife, Elizabeth Barrett, has long been the subject of myth. She began her creative life as a Romantic poet – publishing poems in national newspapers during the 1820s.[8] Her *Sonnets from the Portuguese* (1850) are a remarkable series of love poems which further exploit some of the techniques arising from her husband's dramatic monologues. In fact, they are not 'from the Portuguese' at all; they are original poems that are in some sense autobiographical. The pretence of translation sets up a bluff that allows Barrett Browning to explore her theme without anxiety, sometimes approaching the subject of romantic passion, as experienced by women, quite directly – 'active sexual demands and dangers'.[9] That freedom also licenses her to experiment with different roles, moving easily from that of poet-lover to that of beloved. In *Aurora Leigh* (1856), an experimental (and partly autobiographical) verse-novel that describes the integration of love and work, she set out to challenge more directly the gender discrimination of the day in an effort to formulate a feminist poetic. The extract from the First Book, below (see pp. 9–17), begins this process with a kind of self-portrait written in a reflective, engaging blank verse that in large measure accounts for the resurgence of this work's popularity in recent years.

Emily Brontë is best known as the author of *Wuthering Heights* (1847), but less so as the author of some of the most compelling poetry of the period. Its fascination lies partly in its brooding melancholy and the sense that its author lives in the shadow of some terrible grief in the recent past or anticipation of death to come. The emotional charge of the poetry is intense and often extreme; her subjects are love, hatred, suffering and fortitude. This is particularly evident in such lyrics as 'No coward soul is mine' and 'Cold in the earth'. 'Julian M. and A. G. Rochelle' (known in other versions as 'The Prisoner') is a different kind of poem, at the centre of which is a moment, Rochelle's vision shortly prior to expected death, which allows us to consider Brontë as a mystic writer.

Clough and Arnold knew each other from Oxford days, and are often considered as poets of doubt. This is evident from 'Dover Beach', perhaps Arnold's greatest work, in which he seeks for hope in a 'Sea of Faith', only to turn to human love when faced by a world 'Where ignorant armies clash by night'. 'The Scholar-Gipsy' is one of the great Victorian Oxford poems which tells us a great deal about how important were notions of pastoral at the time. Taking its lead (and diction) from Keats, it contrasts the 'sick hurry' of the world with the comparative calm of the landscape. Clough's agnosticism comes into sharp focus in the two poems presented here, particularly 'That there are powers above us I admit'.

The Victorians were not in themselves a movement, any more than the Romantics, but the Pre-Raphaelite Brotherhood, formed in 1848, was. Of course, like most movements, they were less coherent and unified than they would have liked, and it is easiest to think of the group as one of visual artists. In that context their aim was to introduce the qualities of Italian medieval painting, working directly from the natural object *in situ*, using the colours of nature as they were, and to choose subjects from contemporary life. Where their subject was biblical or historical, they wanted realism, and this often meant introducing 'real' people into the work, and reproducing in

[8]  See for instance 'Stanzas on the Death of Lord Byron', *Romanticism: An Anthology*, 2nd edn, ed. Duncan Wu (Oxford: Blackwell, 2000), pp. 1108–9.

[9]  *Victorian Women Poets: An Anthology* ed. Margaret Reynolds and Angela Leighton (Oxford: Blackwell, 1995), p. 65.

minute detail the features of the natural world. As poets, Dante Gabriel and Christina Rossetti looked back to the Coleridge of 'Christabel' and the Keats of 'Isabella'. In matters of style they sought a simplicity of manner; a sensitivity to sensory detail; a self-conscious medievalism and a highly developed taste in decoration. In mood they cultivated a love of the morbid – listlessness, decay and desolation; and one also finds a frequent use of religious language for evocation (rather than its real meanings). There is in all this a deliberation, a self-consciousness which can sometimes produce startlingly good poetry; it can be found in Tennyson's 'Mariana' and some of the sonnets in Dante Gabriel Rossetti's *House of Life* sequence. 'The Blessed Damozel' (1850) was intended as a companion piece to Poe's 'The Raven' (1845). James Sambrook notes that Rossetti's conception of the afterlife, where the blessed damozel weeps in frustrated longing to join her lover (rather than God) 'is not even remotely Christian'.[10]

Dante Gabriel was to make an art out of the decorativeness and elaboration of his verse; his sister Christina is far less preoccupied with appearances. Her poetry is full of depression and denial, and the intense morbidity of her writing finds expression even in the fairy-tale 'Goblin Market' (1862). Those feelings, which may have deterred some readers in earlier times, have in the last two decades given her work an added resonance, so that in 1995 Margaret Reynolds and Angela Leighton could confirm her place as 'one·of the greatest poets of the nineteenth century'.[11] She is now one of the most widely studied of the Pre-Raphaelites.

Gerard Manley Hopkins's collected verse appeared only in 1918, nearly 30 years after his death, which is why it is easy to regard as a product of the twentieth century. In fact, its 'philological and rhetorical passion'[12] and concentration on the inner workings of the soul is pre-eminently a product of the nineteenth. He is essentially a visionary writer, his concept of 'inscape' referring to the interior perception into the being of the object. Unlike some of the Romantics, Hopkins is insistently religious in his understanding: God is the inscape of the created world. The same cannot be said of the poetry of Hardy, who is also thought of as a twentieth-century writer; indeed, most of his best poetry was written after 1900, published in *Satires of Circumstance* (1914) and *Moments of Vision* (1917). The poems included here are among the best of his Victorian period. Tom Paulin has noted how in 'Neutral Tones' the poem culminates in

> a total picture, an 'involute' or charged combination of emotion and concrete objects, which during his subsequent painful experience has become a permanently meaningful impression.[13]

Not only is there no evidence of religious faith in Hardy's poetry; nature is bleak, as in both 'Neutral Tones' and 'The Darkling Thrush', and capable of blind indifference to human mortality. In this sense it is not fanciful to consider Hardy and Housman alongside each other, except that Housman's vision is if anything even more lacking in hope than Hardy's. In Housman nature is 'heartless, witless', stripped of all the redemptive power with which the Romantics had imbued it, stripped of the religious significance it possessed for such poets as Hopkins.

[10]   'The Rossettis and Other Contemporary Poets', *The Victorians* ed. Arthur Pollard (London: Sphere Books, 1988), p. 438.
[11]   Reynolds and Leighton, *Victorian Women Poets: An Anthology*, p. 355.
[12]   Seamus Heaney, *Preoccupations: Selected Prose 1968–1978* (London: Faber, 1980), p. 85.
[13]   Tom Paulin, *Thomas Hardy: The Poetry of Perception* (London: Macmillan, 1975), p. 31.

This collection of essential poetry of the nineteenth century would appear, then, to trace a course from the sublime hopes of Wordsworth, through the scepticism of Clough, to the outright desolation of Housman and Hardy. Except that it doesn't. Belief may be questioned, but can't be eliminated from the human soul. And in no one was it more vigorously evident than in the work of W. B. Yeats. There have been many fine books about this great writer, but I can't think of a better short guide than Kathleen Raine's *W. B. Yeats and the Learning of the Imagination* (1999). Raine writes of Yeats's place within a fugitive intellectual tradition of metaphysical and mystic thought, a pantheon that includes Thomas Taylor the Platonist, Swedenborg, Plotinus, and the author of the Upanishads:

> Yeats did not study Plato and Plotinus, Swedenborg and Blake, as episodes in the 'history of ideas' but because he was tracing a continuous tradition of knowledge, uncovering the traces of that 'vast generalization' he discerned in the fragmentary portions he assembled. This knowledge is none the less exact and verifiable for being immeasurable; its truth lies in experiences and disciplines of the mind itself and in the testimony (unanimous and worldwide) of 'revelation'.[14]

Never less than exalted in his imaginative ambitions, Yeats's poetry combines the influences of the Pre-Raphaelites, the French symbolists, the kabbalistic and spiritualist worthies with whom he consorted, Irish fairy traditionalism, and nationalist politics in a heady cocktail unlike anything else. 'The Lake Isle of Innisfree' seems like an unexpected way to end a century characterized by increasing doubt and despondency, but in truth the Romantic urge to unify and idealize had never really evaporated. It underpins the medievalism of Tennyson and the Pre-Raphaelites, can be heard beneath the 'tremulous cadence' of the sea in 'Dover Beach', and a longing for it even informs the 'ecstatic sound' of Hardy's darkling thrush (which recalls the 'darkling' experience of Keats's famous ode). Yeats's great poetry, which would produce its finest fruits in the next century, was founded on an unquenchable aspiration, the immortal longings with which the 1800s had begun.

I am much indebted to Valentine Cunningham in what follows, and anyone with a serious interest in this poetry should turn to his anthology, listed below, for fuller scholarly treatment.

## Further Reading

Cunningham, Valentine (ed.) (2000) *The Victorians: An Anthology of Poetry and Poetics* (Oxford: Blackwell.)

Houghton, Walter E. (1957) *The Victorian Frame of Mind, 1830–1870* (New Haven, CT: Yale University Press.)

Reynolds, Margaret and Leighton, Angela (eds) (1995) *Victorian Women Poets: An Anthology* (Oxford: Blackwell.)

Tucker, Herbert F. (ed.) (1999) *A Companion to Victorian Literature and Culture* (Oxford: Blackwell.)

---

[14]  Kathleen Raine, *W. B. Yeats and the Learning of the Imagination* (Ipswich: Golgonooza Press, 1999), p. 76.

# Elizabeth Barrett Browning (1806–1861)

## Sonnets from the Portuguese (extracts)

### XIII

And wilt thou have me fashion into speech
The love I bear thee, finding words enough,
And hold the torch out, while the winds are rough,
Between our faces, to cast light on each! –
I drop it at thy feet. I cannot teach     5
My hand to hold my spirit so far off
From myself... me ... that I should bring thee proof
In words, of love hid in me out of reach.
Nay, let the silence of my womanhood
Commend my woman-love to thy belief, –     10
Seeing that I stand unwon, however wooed,
And rend the garment of my life, in brief,
By a most dauntless, voiceless fortitude,
Lest one touch of this heart convey its grief.

### XVIII

I never gave a lock of hair away
To a man, Dearest, except this to thee,
Which now upon my fingers thoughtfully
I ring out to the full brown length and say
'Take it.' My day of youth went yesterday;     5
My hair no longer bounds to my foot's glee,
Nor plant I it from rose or myrtle-tree,
As girls do, any more. It only may
Now shade on two pale cheeks, the mark of tears,
Taught drooping from the head that hangs aside     10
Through sorrow's trick. I thought the funeral-shears
Would take this first; but Love is justified:
Take it, thou,... finding pure, from all those years,
The kiss my mother left here when she died.

### XXIV

Let the world's sharpness like a clasping knife,
Shut in upon itself and do no harm

In this close hand of Love, now soft and warm;
And let us hear no sound of human strife,
After the click of the shutting. Life to life –                    5
I lean upon thee, Dear, without alarm,
And feel as safe as guarded by a charm,
Against the stab of worldlings who if rife
Are weak to injure. Very whitely still
The lilies of our lives may reassure                               10
Their blossoms from their roots! accessible
Alone to heavenly dews that drop not fewer;
Growing straight, out of man's reach, on the hill.
God only, who made us rich, can make us poor.

### XXXVIII

First time he kissed me, he but only kissed
The fingers of this hand wherewith I write,
And ever since it grew more clean and white, . . .
Slow to world-greetings . . . quick with its 'Oh, list,'
When the angels speak. A ring of amethyst                          5
I could not wear here plainer to my sight,
Than that first kiss. The second passed in height
The first, and sought the forehead, and half missed,
Half falling on the hair. O beyond meed!
That was the chrism of love, which love's own crown,               10
With sanctifying sweetness, did precede.
The third, upon my lips, was folded down
In perfect, purple state! since when, indeed,
I have been proud and said, 'My Love, my own.'

### XLII

How do I love thee? Let me count the ways.
I love thee to the depth and breadth and height
My soul can reach, when feeling out of sight
For the ends of Being and Ideal Grace.
I love thee to the level of everyday's                             5
Most quiet need, by sun and candlelight.
I love thee freely, as men strive for Right;
I love thee purely, as they turn from Praise;
I love thee with the passion put to use
In my old griefs, and with my childhood's faith;                   10
I love thee with a love I seemed to lose
With my lost saints, – I love thee with the breath,
Smiles, tears, of all my life! – and, if God choose,
I shall but love thee better after death.

### XLIII

Beloved, thou hast brought me many flowers
Plucked in the garden, all the summer through

And winter, and it seemed as if they grew
In this close room, nor missed the sun and showers.
So, in the like name of that love of ours,                           5
Take back these thoughts, which here unfolded too,
And which on warm and cold days I withdrew
From my heart's ground. Indeed, those beds and bowers
Be overgrown with bitter weeds and rue,
And wait thy weeding: yet here's eglantine,                         10
Here's ivy! – take them, as I used to do
Thy flowers, and keep them where they shall not pine:
Instruct thine eyes to keep their colours true,
And tell thy soul, their roots are left in mine.

# From *Aurora Leigh*

*Dedication to John Kenyon, Esq.*

The words 'cousin' and 'friend' are constantly recurring in this poem, the last pages of
which have been finished under the hospitality of your roof, my own dearest cousin
and friend; – cousin and friend, in a sense of less equality and greater disinterestedness
than 'Romney''s.

Ending, therefore, and preparing once more to quit England, I venture to leave in
your hands this book, the most mature of my works, and the one into which my
highest convictions upon Life and Art have entered: that as, through my various
efforts in literature and steps in life, you have believed in me, borne with me, and
been generous to me, far beyond the common uses of mere relationship or sympathy
of mind, so you may kindly accept, in sight of the public, this poor sign of esteem,
gratitude, and affection, from

your unforgetting
E. B. B.
39, Devonshire Place,
October 17, 1856

*First Book*

Of writing many books there is no end;
And I who have written much in prose and verse
For others' uses, will write now for mine, –
Will write my story for my better self,
As when you paint your portrait for a friend,                       5
Who keeps it in a drawer and looks at it
Long after he has ceased to love you, just
To hold together what he was and is.

I, writing thus, am still what men call young;
I have not so far left the coasts of life                          10

To travel inland, that I cannot hear
That murmur of the outer Infinite
Which unweaned babies smile at in their sleep
When wondered at for smiling; not so far,
But still I catch my mother at her post                          15
Beside the nursery-door, with finger up,
'Hush, hush – here's too much noise!' while her sweet eyes
Leap forward, taking part against her word
In the child's riot. Still I sit and feel
My father's slow hand, when she had left us both,               20
Stroke out my childish curls across his knee;
And hear Assunta's daily jest (she knew
He liked it better than a better jest)
Inquire how many golden scudi went
To make such ringlets. O my father's hand                      25
Stroke the poor hair down, stroke it heavily, –
Draw, press the child's head closer to thy knee!
I'm still too young, too young, to sit alone.

I write . . . .
                          [. . .]
The cygnet finds the water; but the man                        30
Is born in ignorance of his element,
And feels out blind at first, disorganised
By sin i' the blood, – his spirit-insight dulled
And crossed by his sensations. Presently
We feel it quicken in the dark sometimes;                      35
Then, mark, be reverent, be obedient, –
For those dumb motions of imperfect life
Are oracles of vital Deity
Attesting the Hereafter. Let who says
'The soul's a clean white paper,' rather say,                  40
A palimpsest, a prophet's holograph
Defiled, erased and covered by a monk's, –
The apocalypse, by a Longus! poring on
Which obscene text, we may discern perhaps
Some fair, fine trace of what was written once,                45
Some upstroke of an alpha and omega
Expressing the old scripture.
                          Books, books, books!
I had found the secret of a garret-room
Piled high with cases in my father's name;
Piled high, packed large, – where, creeping in and out         50
Among the giant fossils of my past,
Like some small nimble mouse between the ribs
Of a mastodon, I nibbled here and there
At this or that box, pulling through the gap,
In heats of terror, haste, victorious joy,                     55

The first book first. And how I felt it beat
Under my pillow, in the morning's dark,
An hour before the sun would let me read!
My books!
        At last, because the time was ripe,
I chanced upon the poets.
               As the earth        60
Plunges in fury, when the internal fires
Have reached and pricked her heart, and, throwing flat
The marts and temples, the triumphal gates
And towers of observation, clears herself
To elemental freedom – thus, my soul,        65
At poetry's divine first finger-touch,
Let go conventions and sprang up surprised,
Convicted of the great eternities
Before two worlds.
           What's this, Aurora Leigh,
You write so of the poets, and not laugh?        70
Those virtuous liars, dreamers after dark,
Exaggerators of the sun and moon,
And soothsayers in a teacup?
               I write so
Of the only truth-tellers, now left to God, –
The only speakers of essential truth,        75
Opposed to relative, comparative,
And temporal truths; the only holders by
His sun-skirts, through conventional grey glooms;
The only teachers who instruct mankind,
From just a shadow on a charnel-wall,        80
To find man's veritable stature out,
Erect, sublime, – the measure of a man,
And that's the measure of an angel, says
The apostle. Ay, and while your common men
Build pyramids, gauge railroads, reign, reap, dine,        85
And dust the flaunty carpets of the world
For kings to walk on, or our senators,
The poet suddenly will catch them up
With his voice like a thunder... 'This is soul,
This is life, this word is being said in heaven,        90
Here's God down on us! what are you about?'
How all those workers start amid their work,
Look round, look up, and feel, a moment's space,
That carpet-dusting, though a pretty trade,
Is not the imperative labour after all.        95

My own best poets, am I one with you,
That thus I love you, – or but one through love?
Does all this smell of thyme about my feet

Conclude my visit to your holy hill
In personal presence, or but testify                              100
The rustling of your vesture through my dreams
With influent odours? When my joy and pain,
My thought and aspiration, like the stops
Of pipe or flute, are absolutely dumb
If not melodious, do you play on me,                              105
My pipers, – and if, sooth, you did not blow,
Would no sound come? or is the music mine,
As a man's voice or breath is called his own,
Inbreathed by the Life-breather? There's a doubt
For cloudy seasons!
             But the sun was high                    110
When first I felt my pulses set themselves
For concords; when the rhythmic turbulence
Of blood and brain swept outward upon words,
As wind upon the alders, blanching them
By turning up their under-natures till                            115
They trembled in dilation. O delight
And triumph of the poet, – who would say
A man's mere 'yes,' a woman's common 'no,'
A little human hope of that or this,
And says the word so that it burns you through                   120
With a special revelation, shakes the heart
Of all the men and women in the world,
As if one came back from the dead and spoke,
With eyes too happy, a familiar thing
Become divine i' the utterance! while for him                    125
The poet, the speaker, he expands with joy;
The palpitating angel in his flesh
Thrills inly with consenting fellowship
To those innumerous spirits who sun themselves
Outside of time.
            O life, O poetry,                             130
– Which means life in life! cognisant of life
Beyond this blood-beat, – passionate for truth
Beyond these senses, – poetry, my life, –
My eagle, with both grappling feet still hot
From Zeus's thunder, who has ravished me                         135
Away from all the shepherds, sheep, and dogs,
And set me in the Olympian roar and round
Of luminous faces, for a cup-bearer,
To keep the mouths of all the godheads moist
For everlasting laughters, – I, myself,                          140
Half drunk across the beaker, with their eyes!
How those gods look!
            Enough so, Ganymede.
We shall not bear above a round or two –

We drop the golden cup at Heré's foot
And swoon back to the earth, – and find ourselves          145
Face-down among the pine-cones, cold with dew,
While the dogs bark, and many a shepherd scoffs,
'What's come now to the youth?' Such ups and downs
Have poets.
         Am I such indeed? The name
Is royal, and to sign it like a queen,          150
Is what I dare not, – though some royal blood
Would seem to tingle in me now and then,
With sense of power and ache, – with imposthumes
And manias usual to the race. Howbeit
I dare not: 'tis too easy to go mad,          155
And ape a Bourbon in a crown of straws;
The thing's too common.
             Many fervent souls
Strike rhyme on rhyme, who would strike steel on steel
If steel had offered, in a restless heat
Of doing something. Many tender souls          160
Have strung their losses on a rhyming thread,
As children, cowslips: – the more pains they take,
The work more withers. Young men, ay, and maids,
Too often sow their wild oats in tame verse,
Before they sit down under their own vine          165
And live for use. Alas, near all the birds
Will sing at dawn, – and yet we do not take
The chaffering swallow for the holy lark.

In those days, though, I never analysed
Myself even. All analysis comes late.          170
You catch a sight of Nature, earliest,
In full front sun-face, and your eyelids wink
And drop before the wonder of't; you miss
The form, through seeing the light. I lived, those days,
And wrote because I lived – unlicensed else:          175
My heart beat in my brain. Life's violent flood
Abolished bounds, – and, which my neighbour's field,
Which mine, what mattered? It is so in youth.
We play at leap-frog over the god Term;
The love within us and the love without          180
Are mixed, confounded; if we are loved or love,
We scarce distinguish. So, with other power.
Being acted on and acting seem the same:
In that first onrush of life's chariot-wheels,
We know not if the forests move or we.          185

And so, like most young poets, in a flush
Of individual life, I poured myself

Along the veins of others, and achieved
Mere lifeless imitations of live verse,
And made the living answer for the dead,                    190
Profaning nature. 'Touch not, do not taste,
Nor handle,' – we're too legal, who write young:
We beat the phorminx till we hurt our thumbs,
As if still ignorant of counterpoint;
We call the Muse . . . 'O Muse, benignant Muse!' –          195
As if we had seen her purple-braided head
With the eyes in it, start between the boughs
As often as a stag's. What make-believe,
With so much earnest! what effete results,
From virile efforts! what cold wire-drawn odes,            200
From such white heats! – bucolics, where the cows
Would scare the writer if they splashed the mud
In lashing off the flies, – didactics, driven
Against the heels of what the master said;
And counterfeiting epics, shrill with trumps               205
A babe might blow between two straining cheeks
Of bubbled rose, to make his mother laugh;
And elegiac griefs, and songs of love,
Like cast-off nosegays picked up on the road,
The worse for being warm: all these things, writ          210
On happy mornings, with a morning heart,
That leaps for love, is active for resolve,
Weak for art only. Oft, the ancient forms
Will thrill, indeed, in carrying the young blood.
The wine-skins, now and then, a little warped,            215
Will crack even, as the new wine gurgles in.
Spare the old bottles! – spill not the new wine.

By Keats's soul, the man who never stepped
In gradual progress like another man,
But, turning grandly on his central self,                  220
Ensphered himself in twenty perfect years,
And died, not young, – (the life of a long life,
Distilled to a mere drop, falling like a tear
Upon the world's cold cheek to make it burn
For ever;) by that strong excepted soul,                   225
I count it strange, and hard to understand,
That nearly all young poets should write old;
That Pope was sexagenarian at sixteen,
And beardless Byron academical,
And so with others. It may be, perhaps,                    230
Such have not settled long and deep enough
In trance, to attain to clairvoyance, – and still
The memory mixes with the vision, spoils,
And works it turbid.

Or perhaps, again,
In order to discover the Muse-Sphinx,                          235
The melancholy desert must sweep round,
Behind you, as before. –
            For me, I wrote
False poems, like the rest, and thought them true,
Because myself was true in writing them.
I, peradventure, have writ true ones since                     240
With less complacence.
            But I could not hide
My quickening inner life from those at watch.
They saw a light at a window now and then,
They had not set there. Who had set it there?
My father's sister started when she caught                     245
My soul agaze in my eyes. She could not say
I had no business with a sort of soul,
But plainly she objected, – and demurred,
That souls were dangerous things to carry straight
Through all the spilt saltpetre of the world.                  250

She said sometimes, 'Aurora, have you done
Your task this morning? – have you read that book?
And are you ready for the crochet here?' –
As if she said, 'I know there's something wrong;
I know I have not ground you down enough                       255
To flatten and bake you to a wholesome crust
For household duties and properties,
Before the rain has got into my barn
And set the grains a-sprouting. What, you're green
With out-door impudence? you almost grow?'                     260
To which I answered, 'Would she hear my task,
And verify my abstract of the book?
And should I sit down to the crochet work?
Was such her pleasure?'...Then I sate and teased
The patient needle till it split the thread,                   265
Which oozed off from it in meandering lace
From hour to hour. I was not, therefore, sad;
My soul was singing at a work apart
Behind the wall of sense, as safe from harm
As sings the lark when sucked up out of sight,                 270
In vortices of glory and blue air.

And so, through forced work and spontaneous work,
The inner life informed the outer life,
Reduced the irregular blood to settled rhythms,
Made cool the forehead with fresh-sprinkling dreams,          275
And, rounding to the spheric soul the thin
Pined body, struck a colour up the cheeks,

Though somewhat faint. I clenched my brows across
My blue eyes greatening in the looking-glass,
And said, 'We'll live, Aurora! we'll be strong.                    280
The dogs are on us – but we will not die.'

Whoever lives true life, will love true love.
I learnt to love that England. Very oft,
Before the day was born, or otherwise
Through secret windings of the afternoons,                         285
I threw my hunters off and plunged myself
Among the deep hills, as a hunted stag
Will take the waters, shivering with the fear
And passion of the course. And when, at last
Escaped, – so many a green slope built on slope                    290
Betwixt me and the enemy's house behind,
I dared to rest, or wander, – like a rest
Made sweeter for the step upon the grass, –
And view the ground's most gentle dimplement,
(As if God's finger touched but did not press                      295
In making England!) such an up and down
Of verdure, – nothing too much up or down,
A ripple of land; such little hills, the sky
Can stoop to tenderly and the wheatfields climb;
Such nooks of valleys, lined with orchises,                        300
Fed full of noises by invisible streams;
And open pastures, where you scarcely tell
White daisies from white dew, – at intervals
The mythic oaks and elm-trees standing out
Self-poised upon their prodigy of shade, –                         305
I thought my father's land was worthy too
Of being my Shakspeare's.
                          Very oft alone,
Unlicensed; not unfrequently with leave
To walk the third with Romney and his friend
The rising painter, Vincent Carrington,                            310
Whom men judge hardly, as bee-bonneted,
Because he holds that, paint a body well
You paint a soul by implication, like
The grand first Master. Pleasant walks! for if
He said . . . 'When I was last in Italy' . . .                     315
It sounded as an instrument that's played
Too far off for the tune – and yet it's fine
To listen.
          Ofter we walked only two,
If cousin Romney pleased to walk with me.
We read, or talked, or quarrelled, as it chanced:                  320
We were not lovers, nor even friends well matched –
Say rather, scholars upon different tracks,

And thinkers disagreed; he, overfull
Of what is, and I, haply, overbold
For what might be.
                But then the thrushes sang,      325
And shook my pulses and the elms' new leaves, –
And then I turned, and held my finger up,
And bade him mark that, howsoe'er the world
Went ill, as he related, certainly
The thrushes still sang in it. – At which word     330
His brow would soften, – and he bore with me
In melancholy patience, not unkind,
While, breaking into voluble ecstasy,
I flattered all the beauteous country round,
As poets use . . . the skies, the clouds, the fields,     335
The happy violets hiding from the roads
The primroses run down to, carrying gold, –
The tangled hedgerows, where the cows push out
Impatient horns and tolerant churning mouths
'Twixt dripping ash-boughs, – hedgerows all alive     340
With birds and gnats and large white butterflies
Which look as if the May-flower had caught life
And palpitated forth upon the wind, –
Hills, vales, woods, netted in a silver mist,
Farms, granges, doubled up among the hills,     345
And cattle grazing in the watered vales,
And cottage chimneys smoking from the woods,
And cottage gardens smelling everywhere,
Confused with smell of orchards. 'See,' I said,
'And see! is God not with us on the earth?     350
And shall we put Him down by aught we do?
Who says there's nothing for the poor and vile
Save poverty and wickedness? behold!'
And ankle-deep in English grass I leaped,
And clapped my hands, and called all very fair.     355

In the beginning when God called all good,
Even then was evil near us, it is writ.
But we, indeed, who call things good and fair,
The evil is upon us while we speak:
Deliver us from evil, let us pray.     360

# Alfred (Lord) Tennyson
# (1809–1892)

## Mariana

'Mariana in the moated grange.' – *Measure for Measure*

### I

With blackest moss the flower-plots
   Were thickly crusted, one and all,
The rusted nails fell from the knots
   That held the peach to the garden-wall.
The broken sheds looked sad and strange,      5
   Unlifted was the clinking latch,
   Weeded and worn the ancient thatch
Upon the lonely moated grange.
    She only said 'My life is dreary,
      He cometh not,' she said;      10
    She said 'I am aweary, aweary;
      I would that I were dead!'

### II

Her tears fell with the dews at even;
   Her tears fell ere the dews were dried;
She could not look on the sweet heaven,      15
   Either at morn or eventide.
After the flitting of the bats,
   When thickest dark did trance the sky,
   She drew her casement-curtain by,
And glanced athwart the glooming flats.      20
    She only said 'The night is dreary,
      He cometh not,' she said:
    She said 'I am aweary, aweary,
      I would that I were dead!'

### III

Upon the middle of the night,      25
   Waking she heard the night-fowl crow:
The cock sung out an hour ere light:
   From the dark fen the oxen's low
Came to her: without hope of change,

In sleep she seemed to walk forlorn,                    30
   Till cold winds woke the gray-eyed morn
About the lonely moated grange.
         She only said, 'The day is dreary,
            He cometh not,' she said;
         She said, 'I am aweary, aweary,          35
            I would that I were dead!'

### IV

About a stone-cast from the wall
   A sluice with blackened waters slept,
And o'er it many, round and small,
   The clustered marish-mosses crept.          40
Hard by a poplar shook alway,
   All silver-green with gnarled bark,
   For leagues no other tree did dark
The level waste, the rounding gray.
         She only said, 'My life is dreary,      45
            He cometh not,' she said;
         She said, 'I am aweary, aweary,
            I would that I were dead!'

### V

And ever when the moon was low,
   And the shrill winds were up and away,       50
In the white curtain, to and fro,
   She saw the gusty shadow sway.
But when the moon was very low,
   And wild winds bound within their cell,
   The shadow of the poplar fell                55
Upon her bed, across her brow.
         She only said, 'The night is dreary,
            He cometh not,' she said;
         She said, 'I am aweary, aweary,
            I would that I were dead!'          60

### VI

All day within the dreamy house,
   The doors upon their hinges creaked,
The blue fly sung i' the pane; the mouse
   Behind the mouldering wainscot shrieked,
Or from the crevice peered about.               65
   Old faces glimmered thro' the doors,
   Old footsteps trod the upper floors,
Old voices called her from without.
         She only said, 'My life is dreary,
            He cometh not,' she said;           70
         She said, 'I am aweary, aweary,
            I would that I were dead!'

VII

The sparrow's chirrup on the roof,
    The slow clock ticking, and the sound
Which to the wooing wind aloof         75
    The poplar made, did all confound
Her sense; but most she loathed the hour
    When the thick-moted sunbeam lay
    Athwart the chambers, and the day
Was sloping toward his western bower.    80
        Then, said she, 'I am very dreary,
           He will not come,' she said;
        She wept, 'I am aweary, aweary,
           Oh God, that I were dead!'

# The Lady of Shalott

Part I

On either side the river lie
Long fields of barley and of rye,
That clothe the wold and meet the sky;
And thro' the field the road runs by
    To many-towered Camelot;    5
And up and down the people go,
Gazing where the lilies blow
Round an island there below,
    The island of Shalott.

Willows whiten, aspens quiver,    10
Little breezes dusk and shiver
Thro' the wave that runs for ever
By the island in the river
    Flowing down to Camelot.
Four gray walls, and four gray towers,    15
Overlook a space of flowers,
And the silent isle imbowers
    The Lady of Shalott.

By the margin, willow-veiled,
Slide the heavy barges trailed    20
By slow horses; and unhailed
The shallop flitteth silken-sailed
    Skimming down to Camelot:
But who hath seen her wave her hand?
Or at the casement seen her stand?    25
Or is she known in all the land,
    The Lady of Shalott?

Only reapers, reaping early
In among the bearded barley,
Hear a song that echoes cheerly                                    30
From the river winding clearly,
    Down to towered Camelot:
And by the moon the reaper weary,
Piling sheaves in uplands airy,
Listening, whispers ''Tis the fairy                               35
    Lady of Shalott.'

                    Part II
There she weaves by night and day
A magic web with colours gay.
She has heard a whisper say,
A curse is on her if she stay                                     40
    To look down to Camelot.
She knows not what the curse may be,
And so she weaveth steadily,
And little other care hath she,
    The Lady of Shalott.                                          45

And moving thro' a mirror clear
That hangs before her all the year,
Shadows of the world appear.
There she sees the highway near
    Winding down to Camelot:                                      50
There the river eddy whirls,
And there the surly village-churls,
And the red cloaks of market-girls,
    Pass onward from Shalott.

Sometimes a troop of damsels glad,                                55
An abbot on an ambling pad,
Sometimes a curly shepherd-lad,
Or long-haired page in crimson clad,
    Goes by to towered Camelot;
And sometimes thro' the mirror blue                               60
The knights come riding two and two:
She hath no loyal knight and true,
    The Lady of Shalott.

But in her web she still delights
To weave the mirror's magic sights,                               65
For often thro' the silent nights
A funeral, with plumes and lights
    And music, went to Camelot:
Or when the moon was overhead,
Came two young lovers lately wed;                                 70

'I am half-sick of shadows,' said
   The Lady of Shalott.


       Part III
A bow-shot from her bower-eaves,
He rode between the barley-sheaves,
The sun came dazzling thro' the leaves,        75
And flamed upon the brazen greaves
   Of bold Sir Lancelot.
A redcross knight for ever kneeled
To a lady in his shield,
That sparkled on the yellow field,        80
   Beside remote Shalott.

The gemmy bridle glittered free,
Like to some branch of stars we see
Hung in the golden Galaxy.
The bridle-bells rang merrily        85
   As he rode down to Camelot:
And from his blazoned baldric slung
A mighty silver bugle hung,
And as he rode his armour rung,
   Beside remote Shalott.        90

All in the blue unclouded weather
Thick-jewelled shone the saddle-leather,
The helmet and the helmet-feather
Burned like one burning flame together,
   As he rode down to Camelot.        95
As often thro' the purple night,
Below the starry clusters bright,
Some bearded meteor, trailing light,
   Moves over still Shalott.

His broad clear brow in sunlight glowed;       100
On burnished hooves his war-horse trode;
From underneath his helmet flowed
His coal-black curls as on he rode,
   As he rode down to Camelot.
From the bank and from the river       105
He flashed into the crystal mirror,
'Tirra lirra,' by the river
   Sang Sir Lancelot.

She left the web, she left the loom,
She made three paces thro' the room,       110
She saw the water-lily bloom,
She saw the helmet and the plume,
   She looked down to Camelot.

Out flew the web and floated wide;
The mirror cracked from side to side;                                    115
'The curse is come upon me,' cried
     The Lady of Shalott.

                    Part IV
In the stormy east-wind straining,
The pale yellow woods were waning,
The broad stream in his banks complaining.                               120
Heavily the low sky raining
     Over towered Camelot;
Down she came and found a boat
Beneath a willow left afloat,
And round about the prow she wrote                                       125
     *The Lady of Shalott.*

And down the river's dim expanse –
Like some bold seer in a trance,
Seeing all his own mischance –
With a glassy countenance                                                130
     Did she look to Camelot.
And at the closing of the day
She loosed the chain, and down she lay;
The broad stream bore her far away,
     The Lady of Shalott.                                                135

Lying, robed in snowy white
That loosely flew to left and right –
The leaves upon her falling light –
Thro' the noises of the night
     She floated down to Camelot:                                        140
And as the boat-head wound along
The willowy hills and fields among,
They heard her singing her last song,
     The Lady of Shalott.

Heard a carol, mournful, holy,                                           145
Chanted loudly, chanted lowly,
Till her blood was frozen slowly,
And her eyes were darkened wholly,
     Turned to towered Camelot.
For ere she reached upon the tide                                        150
The first house by the water-side,
Singing in her song she died,
     The Lady of Shalott.

Under tower and balcony,
By garden-wall and gallery,                                              155
A gleaming shape she floated by,

A corse between the houses high,
  Silent into Camelot.
Out upon the wharfs they came,
Knight and burgher, lord and dame,                    160
And round the prow they read her name,
  *The Lady of Shalott.*

Who is this? and what is here?
And in the lighted palace near
Died the sound of royal cheer;                        165
And they crossed themselves for fear,
  All the knights at Camelot:
But Lancelot mused a little space;
He said, 'She has a lovely face;
God in his mercy lend her grace,                      170
  The Lady of Shalott.'

# Ulysses

It little profits that an idle king,
By this still hearth, among these barren crags,
Matched with an aged wife, I mete and dole
Unequal laws unto a savage race,
That hoard, and sleep, and feed, and know not me.     5
I cannot rest from travel: I will drink,
Life to the lees: all times I have enjoyed
Greatly, have suffered greatly, both with those
That loved me, and alone; on shore, and when
Thro' scudding drifts the rainy Hyades               10
Vext the dim sea; I am become a name;
For always roaming with a hungry heart
Much have I seen and known; cities of men
And manners, climates, councils, governments,
Myself not least, but honoured of them all;          15
And drunk delight of battle with my peers,
Far on the ringing plains of windy Troy.
I am a part of all that I have met;
Yet all experience is an arch wherethro'
Gleams that untravelled world, whose margin fades    20
For ever and for ever when I move.
How dull it is to pause, to make an end,
To rust unburnished, not to shine in use!
As tho' to breathe were life. Life piled on life
Were all too little, and of one to me                25
Little remains: but every hour is saved
From that eternal silence, something more,
A bringer of new things; and vile it were

For some three suns to store and hoard myself,
And this gray spirit yearning in desire                              30
To follow knowledge like a sinking star,
Beyond the utmost bound of human thought.
   This is my son, mine own Telemachus,
To whom I leave the sceptre and the isle –
Well-loved of me, discerning to fulfil                               35
This labour, by slow prudence to make mild
A rugged people, and thro' soft degrees
Subdue them to the useful and the good.
Most blameless is he, centred in the sphere
Of common duties, decent not to fail                                 40
In offices of tenderness, and pay
Meet adoration to my household gods,
When I am gone. He works his work, I mine.
   There lies the port; the vessel puffs her sail:
There gloom the dark broad seas. My mariners,                        45
Souls that have toiled, and wrought, and thought with me –
That ever with a frolic welcome took
The thunder and the sunshine, and opposed
Free hearts, free foreheads – you and I are old;
Old age hath yet his honour and his toil;                            50
Death closes all: but something ere the end,
Some work of noble note, may yet be done,
Not unbecoming men that strove with Gods.
The lights begin to twinkle from the rocks:
The long day wanes: the slow moon climbs: the deep                   55
Moans round with many voices. Come, my friends,
'Tis not too late to seek a newer world.
Push off, and, sitting well in order, smite
The sounding furrows; for my purpose holds
To sail beyond the sunset, and the baths                             60
Of all the western stars, until I die.
It may be that the gulfs will wash us down:
It may be we shall touch the Happy Isles,
And see the great Achilles, whom we knew.
Tho' much is taken, much abides; and tho'                            65
We are not now that strength which in old days
Moved earth and heaven; that which we are, we are;
One equal temper of heroic hearts,
Made weak by time and fate, but strong in will
To strive, to seek, to find, and not to yield.                       70

# Morte d'Arthur

So all day long the noise of battle rolled
Among the mountains by the winter sea;

Until King Arthur's table, man by man,
Had fallen in Lyonness about their Lord,
King Arthur: then, because his wound was deep,  5
The bold Sir Bedivere uplifted him,
Sir Bedivere, the last of all his knights,
And bore him to a chapel nigh the field,
A broken chancel with a broken cross,
That stood on a dark strait of barren land.  10
On one side lay the Ocean, and on one
Lay a great water, and the moon was full.
   Then spake King Arthur to Sir Bedivere:
'The sequel of today unsolders all
The goodliest fellowship of famous knights  15
Whereof this world holds record. Such a sleep
They sleep – the men I loved. I think that we
Shall nevermore, at any future time,
Delight our souls with talk of knightly deeds,
Walking about the gardens and the halls  20
Of Camelot, as in the days that were.
I perish by this people which I made, –
Though Merlin sware that I should come again
To rule once more – but let what will be, be,
I am so deeply smitten through the helm  25
That without help I cannot last till morn.
Thou therefore take my brand Excalibur,
Which was my pride: for thou rememberest how
In those old days, one summer noon, an arm
Rose up from out the bosom of the lake,  30
Clothed in white samite, mystic, wonderful,
Holding the sword – and how I rowed across
And took it, and have worn it, like a king:
And, wheresoever I am sung or told
In aftertime, this also shall be known:  35
But now delay not: take Excalibur,
And fling him far into the middle meer:
Watch what thou seest, and lightly bring me word.'
   To him replied the bold Sir Bedivere:
'It is not meet, Sir King, to leave thee thus,  40
Aidless, alone, and smitten through the helm.
A little thing may harm a wounded man.
Yet I thy hest will all perform at full,
Watch what I see, and lightly bring thee word.'
   So saying, from the ruined shrine he stepped,  45
And in the moon athwart the place of tombs,
Where lay the mighty bones of ancient men,
Old knights, and over them the sea-wind sang
Shrill, chill, with flakes of foam. He, stepping down
By zigzag paths, and juts of pointed rock,  50

Came on the shining levels of the lake.
    There drew he forth the brand Excalibur,
And o'er him, drawing it, the winter moon,
Brightening the skirts of a long cloud, ran forth
And sparkled keen with frost against the hilt:                    55
For all the haft twinkled with diamond sparks,
Myriads of topaz-lights, and jacinth-work
Of subtlest jewellery. He gazed so long
That both his eyes were dazzled, as he stood,
This way and that dividing the swift mind,                        60
In act to throw: but at the last it seemed
Better to leave Excalibur concealed
There in the many-knotted waterflags,
That whistled stiff and dry about the marge.
So strode he back slow to the wounded King.                       65
    Then spake King Arthur to Sir Bedivere:
'Hast thou performed my mission which I gave?
What is it thou hast seen? or what hast heard?'
    And answer made the bold Sir Bedivere:
'I heard the ripple washing in the reeds,                         70
And the wild water lapping on the crag.'
    To whom replied King Arthur, faint and pale:
'Thou hast betrayed thy nature and thy name,
Not rendering true answer, as beseemed
Thy fëalty, nor like a noble knight:                              75
For surer sign had followed, either hand,
Or voice, or else a motion of the meer.
This is a shameful thing for men to lie.
Yet now, I charge thee, quickly go again
As thou art lief and dear, and do the thing                      80
I bad thee, watch, and lightly bring me word'.
    Then went Sir Bedivere the second time,
Counting the dewy pebbles, fixed in thought;
But when he saw the wonder of the hilt,
How curiously and strangely chased, he smote                     85
His palms together, and he cried aloud,
    'And if indeed I cast the brand away,
Surely a precious thing, one worthy note,
Should thus be lost for ever from the earth,
Which might have pleased the eyes of many men.                   90
What good should follow this, if this were done?
What harm, undone? deep harm to disobey,
Seeing obedience is the bond of rule.
Were it well to obey then, if a king demand
An act unprofitable, against himself?                            95
The King is sick, and knows not what he does.
What record, or what relic of my lord
Should be to aftertime, but empty breath

And rumours of a doubt? but were this kept,
Stored in some treasure-house of mighty kings,                    100
Some one might show it at a joust of arms,
Saying, 'King Arthur's sword, Excalibur,
Wrought by the lonely maiden of the Lake.
Nine years she wrought it, sitting in the deeps
Upon the hidden bases of the hills.'                              105
So might some old man speak in the aftertime
To all the people, winning reverence.
But now much honour and much fame were lost.'
      So spake he, clouded with his own conceit,
And hid Excalibur the second time,                               110
And so strode back slow to the wounded King.
      Then spoke King Arthur, breathing heavily:
'What is it thou hast seen? or what hast heard?'
      And answer made the bold Sir Bedivere:
'I heard the water lapping on the crag,                          115
And the long ripple washing in the reeds.'
      To whom replied King Arthur, much in wrath:
'Ah, miserable and unkind, untrue,
Unknightly, traitor-hearted! Woe is me!
Authority forgets a dying king,                                 120
Laid widowed of the power in his eye
That bowed the will. I see thee what thou art,
For thou, the latest-left of all my knights,
In whom should meet the offices of all,
Thou wouldst betray me for the precious hilt;                   125
Either from lust of gold, or like a girl
Valuing the giddy pleasure of the eyes.
Yet, for a man may fail in duty twice,
And the third time may prosper, get thee hence:
But, if thou spare to fling Excalibur,                          130
I will arise and slay thee with my hands.'
      Then quickly rose Sir Bedivere, and ran,
And, leaping down the ridges lightly, plunged
Among the bulrush-beds, and clutched the sword,
And strongly wheeled and threw it. The great brand              135
Made lightnings in the splendour of the moon,
And flashing round and round, and whirled in an arch,
Shot like a streamer of the northern morn,
Seen where the moving isles of winter shock
By night, with noises of the northern sea.                      140
So flashed and fell the brand Excalibur:
But ere he dipt the surface, rose an arm
Clothed in white samite, mystic, wonderful,
And caught him by the hilt, and brandished him
Three times, and drew him under in the meer.                    145
And lightly went the other to the King.

Then spoke King Arthur, drawing thicker breath:
'Now see I by thine eyes that this is done.
Speak out: what is it thou hast heard, or seen?'
   And answer made the bold Sir Bedivere:         150
'Sir King, I closed mine eyelids, lest the gems
Should blind my purpose, for I never saw,
Nor shall see, here or elsewhere, till I die,
Not though I live three lives of mortal men,
So great a miracle as yonder hilt.         155
Then with both hands I flung him, wheeling him,
But when I looked again, behold an arm,
Clothed in white samite, mystic, wonderful,
That caught him by the hilt, and brandished him
Three times, and drew him under in the meer.'        160
   And answer made King Arthur, breathing hard:
'My end draws nigh; 'tis time that I were gone.
Make broad thy shoulders to receive my weight,
And bear me to the margin; yet I fear
My wound hath taken cold, and I shall die.'        165
   So saying, from the pavement he half rose,
Slowly, with pain, reclining on his arm,
And looking wistfully with wide blue eyes
As in a picture. Him Sir Bedivere
Remorsefully regarded thro' his tears,        170
And would have spoken, but he found not words,
Then took with care, and kneeling on one knee,
O'er both his shoulders drew the languid hands,
And rising bore him thro' the place of tombs.
   But, as he walked, King Arthur panted hard,        175
Like one that feels a nightmare on his bed
When all the house is mute. So sighed the King,
Muttering and murmuring at his ear, 'Quick, quick!
I fear it is too late, and I shall die.'
But the other swiftly strode from ridge to ridge,        180
Clothed with his breath, and looking, as he walked,
Larger than human on the frozen hills.
He heard the deep behind him, and a cry
Before. His own thought drove him like a goad.
Dry clashed his harness in the icy caves        185
And barren chasms, and all to left and right
The bare black cliff clanged round him, as he based
His feet on juts of slippery crag that rang
Sharp-smitten with the dint of armed heels –
And on a sudden, lo! the level lake,        190
And the long glories of the winter moon.
   Then saw they how there hove a dusky barge,
Dark as a funeral scarf from stem to stern,
Beneath them; and descending they were ware

That all the decks were dense with stately forms                    195
Black-stoled, black-hooded, like a dream – by these
Three Queens with crowns of gold – and from them rose
A cry that shivered to the tingling stars,
And, as it were one voice, an agony
Of lamentation, like a wind, that shrills                           200
All night in a waste land, where no one comes,
Or hath come, since the making of the world.
    Then murmured Arthur, 'Place me in the barge,'
And to the barge they came. There those three Queens
Put forth their hands, and took the King, and wept.                 205
But she, that rose the tallest of them all
And fairest, laid his head upon her lap,
And loosed the shattered casque, and chafed his hands,
And called him by his name, complaining loud,
And dropping bitter tears against his brow                         210
Striped with dark blood: for all his face was white
And colourless, and like the withered moon
Smote by the fresh beam of the springing east;
And all his greaves and cuisses dashed with drops
Of onset; and the light and lustrous curls –                       215
That made his forehead like a rising sun
High from the dais-throne – were parched with dust;
Or, clotted into points and hanging loose,
Mixed with the knightly growth that fringed his lips.
So like a shattered column lay the King;                           220
Not like that Arthur who, with lance in rest,
From spur to plume a star of tournament,
Shot thro' the lists at Camelot, and charged
Before the eyes of ladies and of kings.
    Then loudly cried the bold Sir Bedivere,                        225
'Ah! my Lord Arthur, whither shall I go?
Where shall I hide my forehead and my eyes?
For now I see the true old times are dead,
When every morning brought a noble chance,
And every chance brought out a noble knight.                       230
Such times have been not since the light that led
The holy Elders with the gift of myrrh.
But now the whole ROUND TABLE is dissolved
Which was an image of the mighty world;
And I, the last, go forth companionless,                           235
And the days darken round me, and the years,
Among new men, strange faces, other minds.'
    And slowly answered Arthur from the barge:
'The old order changeth, yielding place to new,
And God fulfils Himself in many ways,                              240
Lest one good custom should corrupt the world.
Comfort thyself: what comfort is in me?

I have lived my life, and that which I have done
May He within Himself make pure! but thou –
If thou shouldst never see my face again,                              245
Pray for my soul. More things are wrought by prayer
Than this world dreams of. Wherefore, let thy voice
Rise like a fountain for me night and day.
For what are men better than sheep or goats
That nourish a blind life within the brain,                             250
If, knowing God, they lift not hands of prayer
Both for themselves and those who call them friend?
For so the whole round earth is every way
Bound by gold chains about the feet of God.
But now farewell. I am going a long way                                255
With these thou seest – if indeed I go –
(For all my mind is clouded with a doubt)
To the island-valley of Avilion;
Where falls not hail, or rain, or any snow,
Nor ever wind blows loudly; but it lies                                260
Deep-meadowed, happy, fair with orchard-lawns
And bowery hollows crowned with summer sea,
Where I will heal me of my grievous wound.'
    So said he, and the barge with oar and sail
Moved from the brink, like some full-breasted swan                     265
That, fluting a wild carol ere her death,
Ruffles her pure cold plume, and takes the flood
With swarthy webs. Long stood Sir Bedivere
Revolving many memories, till the hull
Looked one black dot against the verge of dawn,                        270
And on the meer the wailing died away.

Here ended Hall, and our last light, that long
Had winked and threatened darkness, flared and fell:
At which the Parson, sent to sleep with sound,
And waked with silence, grunted 'Good!' but we                         275
Sat rapt: it was the tone with which he read –
Perhaps some modern touches here and there
Redeemed it from the charge of nothingness –
Or else we loved the man, and prized his work;
I know not: but we sitting, as I said,                                 280
The cock crew loud; as at that time of year
The lusty bird takes every hour for dawn:
Then Francis, muttering, like a man ill-used,
'There now – that's nothing!' drew a little back,
And drove his heel into the smouldered log,                            285
That sent a blast of sparkles up the flue:
And so to bed; where yet in sleep I seemed
To sail with Arthur under looming shores,
Point after point; till on to dawn, when dreams

Begin to feel the truth and stir of day,                                    290
To me, methought, who waited with a crowd,
There came a bark that, blowing forward, bore
King Arthur, like a modern gentleman
Of stateliest port; and all the people cried,
'Arthur is come again: he cannot die.'                                      295
Then those that stood upon the hills behind
Repeated – 'Come again, and thrice as fair;'
And, further inland, voices echoed – 'Come
With all good things, and war shall be no more.'
At this a hundred bells began to peal,                                      300
That with the sound I woke, and heard indeed
The clear church-bells ring in the Christmas-morn.

## 'Break, Break, Break'

Break, break, break,
    On thy cold gray stones, O Sea!
And I would that my tongue could utter
    The thoughts that arise in me.

O well for the fisherman's boy,                                             5
    That he shouts with his sister at play!
O well for the sailor lad,
    That he sings in his boat on the bay!

And the stately ships go on
    To their haven under the hill;                                         10
But O for the touch of a vanished hand,
    And the sound of a voice that is still!

Break, break, break,
    At the foot of thy crags, O Sea!
But the tender grace of a day that is dead                                  15
    Will never come back to me.

## From: The Princess; A Medley

Tears, idle tears, I know not what they mean,
Tears from the depth of some divine despair
Rise in the heart, and gather to the eyes,
In looking on the happy Autumn-fields,
And thinking of the days that are no more.                                  5

Fresh as the first beam glittering on a sail,
That brings our friends up from the underworld,

Sad as the last which reddens over one
That sinks with all we love below the verge;
So sad, so fresh, the days that are no more.                    10

Ah, sad and strange as in dark summer dawns
The earliest pipe of half-awakened birds
To dying ears, when unto dying eyes
The casement slowly grows a glimmering square;
So sad, so strange, the days that are no more.                 15

Dear as remembered kisses after death,
And sweet as those by hopeless fancy feigned
On lips that are for others; deep as love,
Deep as first love, and wild with all regret;
O Death in Life, the days that are no more.                    20

    . . . .

Now sleeps the crimson petal, now the white;
Nor waves the cypress in the palace walk;
Nor winks the gold fin in the porphyry font:
The fire-fly wakens: waken thou with me.

  Now droops the milkwhite peacock like a ghost,     5
And like a ghost she glimmers on to me.
  Now lies the Earth all Danaë to the stars,
And all thy heart lies open unto me.

  Now slides the silent meteor on, and leaves
A shining furrow, as thy thoughts in me.                       10

  Now folds the lily all her sweetness up,
And slips into the bosom of the lake:
So fold thyself, my dearest, thou, and slip
Into my bosom and be lost in me.

    . . . .

Come down, O maid, from yonder mountain height:
What pleasure lives in height (the shepherd sang)
In height and cold, the splendour of the hills?
But cease to move so near the Heavens, and cease
To glide a sunbeam by the blasted Pine,                        5
To sit a star upon the sparkling spire;
And come, for Love is of the valley, come,
For Love is of the valley, come thou down
And find him; by the happy threshold, he,
Or hand in hand with Plenty in the maize,                      10
Or red with spirted purple of the vats,
Or foxlike in the vine; nor cares to walk
With Death and Morning on the Silver Horns,
Nor wilt thou snare him in the white ravine,
Nor find him dropt upon the firths of ice,                     15

That huddling slant in furrow-cloven falls
To roll the torrent out of dusky doors:
But follow; let the torrent dance thee down
To find him in the valley; let the wild
Lean-headed Eagles yelp alone, and leave                    20
The monstrous ledges there to slope, and spill
Their thousand wreaths of dangling water-smoke,
That like a broken purpose waste in air:
So waste not thou; but come; for all the vales
Await thee; azure pillars of the hearth                     25
Arise to thee; the children call, and I
Thy shepherd pipe, and sweet is every sound,
Sweeter thy voice, but every sound is sweet;
Myriads of rivulets hurrying thro' the lawn,
The moan of doves in immemorial elms,                       30
And murmuring of innumerable bees.

## From *In Memoriam* A. H. H.

Strong Son of God, immortal Love,
   Whom we, that have not seen thy face,
   By faith, and faith alone, embrace,
Believing where we cannot prove;

Thine are these orbs of light and shade;                    5
   Thou madest Life in man and brute;
   Thou madest Death; and lo, thy foot
Is on the skull which thou hast made.

Thou wilt not leave us in the dust:
   Thou madest man, he knows not why;                 10
   He thinks he was not made to die;
And thou hast made him: thou art just.

Thou seemest human and divine,
   The highest, holiest manhood, thou:
   Our wills are ours, we know not how;               15
Our wills are ours, to make them thine.

Our little systems have their day;
   They have their day and cease to be:
   They are but broken lights of thee,
And thou, O Lord, art more than they.                       20

We have but faith: we cannot know;
   For knowledge is of things we see;
   And yet we trust it comes from thee,
A beam in darkness: let it grow.

Let knowledge grow from more to more,                    25
    But more of reverence in us dwell;
    That mind and soul, according well,
May make one music as before,

But vaster. We are fools and slight;
    We mock thee when we do not fear:                    30
    But help thy foolish ones to bear;
Help thy vain worlds to bear thy light.

Forgive what seemed my sin in me;
    What seemed my worth since I began;
    For merit lives from man to man,                     35
And not from man, O Lord, to thee.

Forgive my grief for one removed,
    Thy creature, whom I found so fair.
    I trust he lives in thee, and there
I find him worthier to be loved.                         40

Forgive these wild and wandering cries,
    Confusions of a wasted youth;
    Forgive them where they fail in truth,
And in thy wisdom make me wise.
                                    1849

# In Memoriam

### A. H. H.

#### OBIIT MDCCCXXXIII

### I

I held it truth, with him who sings
    To one clear harp in divers tones,
    That men may rise on stepping-stones
Of their dead selves to higher things.

But who shall so forecast the years                      5
    And find in loss a gain to match?
    Or reach a hand thro' time to catch
The far-off interest of tears?

Let Love clasp Grief lest both be drowned,
    Let darkness keep her raven gloss:                   10
    Ah! sweeter to be drunk with loss,
To dance with death, to beat the ground;

Than that the victor Hours should scorn
   The long result of love, and boast:
     'Behold the man that loved and lost,          15
But all he was is overworn.'

### II

Old Yew, which graspest at the stones
   That name the under-lying dead,
   Thy fibres net the dreamless head;
Thy roots are wrapt about the bones.

The seasons bring the flower again,          5
   And bring the firstling to the flock;
   And in the dusk of thee, the clock
Beats out the little lives of men.

O! not for thee the glow, the bloom,
   Who changest not in any gale!          10
   Nor branding summer suns avail
To touch thy thousand years of gloom.

And gazing on the sullen tree,
   Sick for thy stubborn hardihood,
   I seem to fail from out my blood          15
And grow incorporate into thee.

### III

O Sorrow, cruel fellowship!
   O Priestess in the vaults of Death!
   O sweet and bitter in a breath,
What whispers from thy lying lip?

'The stars,' she whispers, 'blindly run;          5
   A web is woven across the sky;
   From out waste places comes a cry,
And murmurs from the dying sun:

'And all the phantom, Nature, stands –
   With all the music in her tone,          10
   A hollow echo of my own, –
A hollow form with empty hands.'

And shall I take a thing so blind,
   Embrace her as my natural good;
   Or crush her, like a vice of blood,          15
Upon the threshold of the mind?

IV

To Sleep I give my powers away;
    My will is bondsman to the dark;
    I sit within a helmless bark,
And with my heart I muse and say:

O heart, how fares it with thee now,                                5
    That thou should'st fail from thy desire,
    Who scarcely darest to inquire,
'What is it makes me beat so low?'

Something it is which thou hast lost,
    Some pleasure from thine early years.                          10
    Break, thou deep vase of chilling tears,
That grief hath shaken into frost!

Such clouds of nameless trouble cross
    All night below the darkened eyes;
    With morning wakes the will, and cries,                        15
'Thou shalt not be the fool of loss.'

V

I sometimes hold it half a sin
    To put in words the grief I feel;
    For words, like nature, half reveal
And half conceal the Soul within.

But, for the unquiet heart and brain,                              5
    A use in measured language lies;
    The sad mechanic exercise,
Like dull narcotics, numbing pain.

In words, like weeds, I'll wrap me o'er,
    Like coarsest clothes against the cold;                        10
    But that large grief which these enfold
Is given in outline and no more.

VI

One writes, that 'Other friends remain,'
    That 'Loss is common to the race' –
    And common is the commonplace,
And vacant chaff well meant for grain.

That loss is common would not make                                 5
    My own less bitter, rather more:
    Too common! Never morning wore
To evening, but some heart did break.

O father, wheresoe'er thou be,
　　That pledgest now thy gallant son;　　　　　　　　10
　　A shot, ere half thy draught be done
Hath stilled the life that beat from thee.

O mother, praying God will save
　　Thy sailor, – while thy head is bowed,
　　His heavy-shotted hammock-shroud　　　　　　　15
Drops in his vast and wandering grave.

Ye know no more than I who wrought
　　At that last hour to please him well;
　　Who mused on all I had to tell,
And something written, something thought;　　　　　20

Expecting still his advent home;
　　And ever met him on his way
　　With wishes, thinking, here today,
Or here tomorrow will he come.

O! somewhere, meek, unconscious dove,　　　　　　25
　　That sittest ranging golden hair;
　　And glad to find thyself so fair,
Poor child, that waitest for thy love!

For now her father's chimney glows
　　In expectation of a guest;　　　　　　　　　　　30
　　And thinking 'this will please him best,'
She takes a riband or a rose;

For he will see them on to-night;
　　And with the thought her colour burns;
　　And, having left the glass, she turns　　　　　　35
Once more to set a ringlet right;

And, even when she turned, the curse
　　Had fallen, and her future Lord
　　Was drowned in passing thro' the ford,
Or killed in falling from his horse.　　　　　　　　40

O, what to her shall be the end?
　　And what to me remains of good?
　　To her, perpetual maidenhood,
And unto me no second friend.

### VII

Dark house, by which once more I stand
　　Here in the long unlovely street,
　　Doors, where my heart was used to beat
So quickly, waiting for a hand,

A hand that can be clasped no more –                                5
  Behold me, for I cannot sleep,
  And like a guilty thing I creep
At earliest morning to the door.

He is not here; but far away
  The noise of life begins again,                                   10
  And ghastly thro' the drizzling rain
On the bald street breaks the blank day.

### VIII

A happy lover who has come
  To look on her that loves him well,
  Who lights and rings the gateway bell,
And learns her gone and far from home;

He saddens, all the magic light                                     5
  Dies off at once from bower and hall,
  And all the place is dark, and all
The chambers emptied of delight;

So find I every pleasant spot
  In which we two were wont to meet,                                10
  The field, the chamber and the street,
For all is dark where thou art not.

Yet as that other, wandering there
  In those deserted walks, may find
  A flower beat with rain and wind,                                 15
Which once she fostered up with care;

So seems it in my deep regret,
  O my forsaken heart, with thee
  And this poor flower of poesy
Which little cared for fades not yet.                               20

But since it pleased a vanished eye,
  I go to plant it on his tomb,
  That if it can it there may bloom,
Or dying, there at least may die.

### IX

Fair ship, that from the Italian shore
  Sailest the placid ocean-plains
  With my lost Arthur's loved remains,
Spread thy full wings, and waft him o'er.

So draw him home to those that mourn                                5
  In vain; a favourable speed

Ruffle thy mirrored mast, and lead
Thro' prosperous floods his holy urn.

All night no ruder air perplex
   Thy sliding keel, till Phosphor,[1] bright      10
   As our pure love, thro' early light
Shall glimmer on the dewy decks.

Sphere all your lights around, above;
   Sleep, gentle heavens, before the prow;
   Sleep, gentle winds, as he sleeps now,      15
My friend, the brother of my love;

My Arthur, whom I shall not see
   Till all my widowed race be run;
   Dear as the mother to the son,
More than my brothers are to me.      20

X

I hear the noise about thy keel;
   I hear the bell struck in the night:
   I see the cabin-window bright;
I see the sailor at the wheel.

Thou bringest the sailor to his wife,      5
   And travelled men from foreign lands;
   And letters unto trembling hands;
And, thy dark freight, a vanished life.

So bring him: we have idle dreams:
   This look of quiet flatters thus      10
   Our home-bred fancies: O to us,
The fools of habit, sweeter seems

To rest beneath the clover sod,
   That takes the sunshine and the rains,
   Or where the kneeling hamlet drains      15
The chalice of the grapes of God;

Than if with thee the roaring wells
   Should gulf him fathom-deep in brine;
   And hands so often clasped in mine,
Should toss with tangle[2] and with shells.      20

XI

Calm is the morn without a sound,
   Calm as to suit a calmer grief,

[1]  'star of dawn' (T.).
[2]  'oar-weed' (T.).

And only thro' the faded leaf
The chestnut pattering to the ground:

Calm and deep peace on this high wold,                    5
    And on these dews that drench the furze,
    And all the silvery gossamers
That twinkle into green and gold:

Calm and still light on yon great plain
    That sweeps with all its autumn bowers,               10
    And crowded farms and lessening towers,
To mingle with the bounding main:

Calm and deep peace in this wide air,
    These leaves that redden to the fall;
    And in my heart, if calm at all,                      15
If any calm, a calm despair:

Calm on the seas, and silver sleep,
    And waves that sway themselves in rest,
    And dead calm in that noble breast
Which heaves but with the heaving deep.                   20

### XII

Lo! as a dove when up she springs
    To bear thro' Heaven a tale of woe,
    Some dolorous message knit below
The wild pulsation of her wings;

Like her I go; I cannot stay;                             5
    I leave this mortal ark behind,
    A weight of nerves without a mind,
And leave the cliffs, and haste away

O'er ocean-mirrors rounded large,
    And reach the glow of southern skies,                 10
    And see the sails at distance rise,
And linger weeping on the marge,

And saying; 'Comes he thus, my friend?
    Is this the end of all my care?'
    And circle moaning in the air:                        15
'Is this the end? Is this the end?'

And forward dart again, and play
    About the prow, and back return
    To where the body sits, and learn
That I have been an hour away.                            20

### XIII

Tears of the widower, when he sees
   A late-lost form that sleep reveals,
   And moves his doubtful arms, and feels
Her place is empty, fall like these;

Which weep a loss for ever new,              5
   A void where heart on heart reposed;
   And, where warm hands have prest and closed,
Silence, till I be silent too.

Which weep the comrade of my choice,
   An awful thought, a life removed,          10
   The human-hearted man I loved,
A spirit, not a breathing voice.

Come Time, and teach me, many years,
   I do not suffer in a dream;
   For now so strange do these things seem,     15
Mine eyes have leisure for their tears;

My fancies time to rise on wing,
   And glance about the approaching sails,
   As tho' they brought but merchants' bales,
And not the burthen that they bring.          20

### XIV

If one should bring me this report,
   That thou hadst touched the land today,
   And I went down unto the quay,
And found thee lying in the port,

And standing, muffled round with woe,     5
   Should see thy passengers in rank
   Come stepping lightly down the plank,
And beckoning unto those they know,

And if along with these should come
   The man I held as half-divine;
   Should strike a sudden hand in mine,     10
And ask a thousand things of home;

And I should tell him all my pain,
   And how my life had dropped of late,
   And he should sorrow o'er my state
And marvel what possessed my brain;     15

And I perceived no touch of change,
   No hint of death in all his frame,
   But found him all in all the same,
I should not feel it to be strange.        20

### XV

To-night the winds begin to rise
   And roar from yonder dropping day:
   The last red leaf is whirled away,
The rooks are blown about the skies;

The forest cracked, the waters curled,        5
   The cattle huddled on the lea;
   And wildly dashed on tower and tree
The sunbeam strikes along the world:

And but for fancies, which aver
   That all thy motions gently pass        10
   Athwart a plane of molten glass,
I scarce could brook the strain and stir

That makes the barren branches loud;
   And but for fear it is not so,
   The wild unrest that lives in woe        15
Would dote and pore on yonder cloud

That rises upward always higher,
   And onward drags a labouring breast,
   And topples round the dreary west,
A looming bastion fringed with fire.        20

### XVI

What words are these have fallen from me?
   Can calm despair and wild unrest
   Be tenants of a single breast,
Or sorrow such a changeling be?

Or doth she only seem to take        5
   The touch of change in calm or storm;
   But knows no more of transient form
In her deep self, than some dead lake

That holds the shadow of a lark
   Hung in the shadow of a heaven?        10
   Or has the shock, so harshly given,
Confused me like the unhappy bark

That strikes by night a craggy shelf,
   And staggers blindly ere she sink?

And stunned me from my power to think 15
And all my knowledge of myself;

And made me that delirious man
  Whose fancy fuses old and new,
  And flashes into false and true,
And mingles all without a plan? 20

### XVII

Thou comest, much wept for: such a breeze
  Compelled thy canvas, and my prayer
  Was as the whisper of an air
To breathe thee over lonely seas.

For I in spirit saw thee move 5
  Thro' circles of the bounding sky;
  Week after week: the days go by:
Come quick, thou bringest all I love.

Henceforth, wherever thou may'st roam,
  My blessing, like a line of light,
  Is on the waters day and night, 10
And like a beacon guards thee home.

So may whatever tempest mars
  Mid-ocean, spare thee, sacred bark;
  And balmy drops in summer dark 15
Slide from the bosom of the stars.

So kind an office hath been done,
  Such precious relics brought by thee;
  The dust of him I shall not see
Till all my widowed race be run. 20

### XVIII

'Tis well; 'tis something, we may stand
  Where he in English earth is laid,
  And from his ashes may be made
The violet of his native land.

'Tis little; but it looks in truth 5
  As if the quiet bones were blest
  Among familiar names to rest
And in the places of his youth.

Come then, pure hands, and bear the head
  That sleeps or wears the mask of sleep,
  And come, whatever loves to weep, 10
And hear the ritual of the dead.

Ah! yet, even yet, if this might be,
   I, falling on his faithful heart,
   Would breathing thro' his lips impart        15
The life that almost dies in me:

That dies not, but endures with pain,
   And slowly forms the firmer mind,
   Treasuring the look it cannot find,
The words that are not heard again.        20

## XIX

The Danube to the Severn gave
   The darkened heart that beat no more;[3]
   They laid him by the pleasant shore,
And in the hearing of the wave.

There twice a day the Severn fills,        5
   The salt sea-water passes by,
   And hushes half the babbling Wye,
And makes a silence in the hills.

The Wye is hushed nor moved along;
   And hushed my deepest grief of all,        10
   When filled with tears that cannot fall,
I brim with sorrow drowning song.

The tide flows down, the wave again
   Is vocal in its wooded walls:
   My deeper anguish also falls,        15
And I can speak a little then.

## XX

The lesser griefs that may be said,
   That breathe a thousand tender vows,
   Are but as servants in a house
Where lies the master newly dead;

Who speak their feeling as it is,        5
   And weep the fulness from the mind:
   'It will be hard,' they say, 'to find
Another service such as this.'

My lighter moods are like to these,
   That out of words a comfort win;        10
   But there are other griefs within,
And tears that at their fountain freeze;

---

[3] 'He died at Vienna and was brought to Clevedon to be buried' (T.).

For by the hearth the children sit
   Cold in that atmosphere of Death,
   And scarce endure to draw the breath.             15
Or like to noiseless phantoms flit:

But open converse is there none,
   So much the vital spirits sink
   To see the vacant chair, and think,
'How good! how kind! and he is gone.'         20

### XXI

I sing to him that rests below,
   And, since the grasses round me wave,
   I take the grasses of the grave,
And make them pipes whereon to blow.

The traveller hears me now and then,         5
   And sometimes harshly will he speak;
   'This fellow would make weakness weak,
And melt the waxen hearts of men.'

Another answers, 'Let him be,
   He loves to make parade of pain,         10
   That with his piping he may gain
The praise that comes to constancy.'

A third is wroth: 'Is this an hour
   For private sorrow's barren song,
   When more and more the people throng      15
The chairs and thrones of civil power?

'A time to sicken and to swoon,
   When science reaches forth her arms
   To feel from world to world, and charms
Her secret from the latest moon?'         20

Behold, ye speak an idle thing:
   Ye never knew the sacred dust:
   I do but sing because I must,
And pipe but as the linnets sing:

And one unto her note is gay,         25
   For now her little ones have ranged;
   And one unto her note is changed,
Because her brood is stol'n away.

### XXII

The path by which we twain did go,
   Which led by tracts that pleased us well,

Thro' four sweet years arose and fell,
From flower to flower, from snow to snow:

And we with singing cheered the way,                                    5
    And crowned with all the season lent,
    From April on to April went,
And glad at heart from May to May:

But where the path we walked began
    To slant the fifth autumnal slope,                                  10
    As we descended following Hope,
There sat the Shadow feared of man;

Who broke our fair companionship,
    And spread his mantle dark and cold;
    And wrapt thee formless in the fold,                                15
And dulled the murmur on thy lip;

And bore thee where I could not see
    Nor follow, tho' I walk in haste;
    And think that, somewhere in the waste,
The Shadow sits and waits for me.                                       20

XXIII

Now, sometimes in my sorrow shut,
    Or breaking into song by fits,
    Alone, alone, to where he sits,
The Shadow cloaked from head to foot

Who keeps the keys of all the creeds,                                   5
    I wander, often falling lame,
    And looking back to whence I came,
Or on to where the pathway leads;

And crying, how changed from where it ran
    Thro' lands where not a leaf was dumb;                              10
    But all the lavish hills would hum
The murmur of a happy Pan:

When each by turns was guide to each,
    And Fancy light from Fancy caught,
    And Thought leapt out to wed with Thought,                         15
Ere thought could wed itself with Speech;

And all we met was fair and good,
    And all was good that Time could bring,
    And all the secret of the Spring
Moved in the chambers of the blood:                                     20

And many an old philosophy
   On Argive heights divinely sang,
   And round us all the thicket rang
To many a flute of Arcady.

### XXIV

And was the day of my delight
   As pure and perfect as I say?
   The very source and fount of Day
Is dashed with wandering isles of night.

If all was good and fair we met,       5
   This earth had been the Paradise
   It never looked to human eyes
Since Adam left his garden yet.

And is it that the haze of grief
   Hath stretched my former joy so great?       10
   The lowness of the present state,
That sets the past in this relief?

Or that the past will always win
   A glory from its being far;
   And orb into the perfect star       15
We saw not, when we moved therein?

### XXV

I know that this was Life, – the track
   Whereon with equal feet we fared;
   And then, as now, the day prepared
The daily burden for the back.

But this it was that made me move       5
   As light as carrier-birds in air;
   I loved the weight I had to bear,
Because it needed help of Love:

Nor could I weary, heart or limb,
   When mighty Love would cleave in twain       10
   The lading of a single pain,
And part it, giving half to him.

### XXVI

Still onward winds the dreary way;
   I with it; for I long to prove
   No lapse of moons can canker Love,
Whatever fickle tongues may say.

And if that eye which watches guilt       5
   And goodness, and hath power to see

Within the green the mouldered tree,
And towers fallen as soon as built –

Oh, if indeed that eye foresee
   Or see (in Him is no before)           10
   In more of life true life no more
And Love the indifference to be,

So might I find, ere yet the morn
   Breaks hither over Indian seas,
   That Shadow waiting with the keys,      15
To cloak me from my proper scorn.

### XXVII

I envy not in any moods
   The captive void of noble rage,
   The linnet born within the cage
That never knew the summer woods:

I envy not the beast that takes         5
   His license in the field of time,
   Unfettered by the sense of crime,
To whom a conscience never wakes;

Nor, what may count itself as blest,
   The heart that never plighted troth      10
   But stagnates in the weeds of sloth;
Nor any want-begotten rest.

I hold it true, whate'er befall;
   I feel it, when I sorrow most;
   'Tis better to have loved and lost      15
Than never to have loved at all.

### XLI

Thy spirit ere our fatal loss
   Did ever rise from high to higher;
   As mounts the heavenward altar-fire,
As flies the lighter thro' the gross.

But thou art turned to something strange,      5
   And I have lost the links that bound
   Thy changes; here upon the ground;
No more partaker of thy change.

Deep folly! yet that this could be –
   That I could wing my will with might      10
   To leap the grades of life and light,
And flash at once, my friend, to thee:

For though my nature rarely yields
    To that vague fear implied in death;
    Nor shudders at the gulfs beneath,         15
The howlings from forgotten fields;

Yet oft when sundown skirts the moor
    An inner trouble I behold,
    A spectral doubt which makes me cold,
That I shall be thy mate no more,         20

Tho' following with an upward mind
    The wonders that have come to thee,
    Thro' all the secular to be,
But evermore a life behind.

### XLVIII

If these brief lays, of Sorrow born,
    Were taken to be such as closed
    Grave doubts and answers here proposed,
Then these were such as men might scorn:

Her care is not to part and prove;         5
    She takes, when harsher moods remit,
    What slender shade of doubt may flit,
And makes it vassal unto love:

And hence, indeed, she sports with words;
    But better serves a wholesome law,         10
    And holds it sin and shame to draw
The deepest measure from the chords:

Nor dare she trust a larger lay,
    But rather loosens from the lip
    Short swallow-flights of song, that dip         15
Their wings in tears, and skim away.

### XLIX

From art, from nature, from the schools,
    Let random influences glance,
    Like light in many a shivered lance
That breaks about the dappled pools:

The lightest wave of thought shall lisp,         5
    The fancy's tenderest eddy wreathe,
    The slightest air of song shall breathe
To make the sullen surface crisp.

And look thy look, and go thy way,
    but blame not thou the winds that make         10

The seeming-wanton ripple break,
The tender-pencilled shadow play.

Beneath all fancied hopes and fears
   Ay me! the sorrow deepens down,
   Whose muffled motions blindly drown      15
The bases of my life in tears.

### LIV

Oh yet we trust that somehow good
   Will be the final goal of ill,
   To pangs of nature, sins of will,
Defects of doubt, and taints of blood;

That nothing walks with aimless feet;      5
   That not one life shall be destroyed,
   Or cast as rubbish to the void,
When God hath made the pile complete;

That not a worm is cloven in vain;
   That not a moth with vain desire      10
   Is shriveled in a fruitless fire,
Or but subserves another's gain.

Behold! we know not anything;
   I can but trust that good shall fall
   At last – far off – at last, to all,      15
And every winter change to spring.

So runs my dream: but what am I?
   An infant crying in the night:
   An infant crying for the light:
And with no language but a cry.      20

### LV

The wish, that of the living whole
   No life may fail beyond the grave;
   Derives it not from what we have
The likest God within the soul?

Are God and Nature then at strife,      5
   That Nature lends such evil dreams?
   So careful of the type she seems,
So careless of the single life;

That I, considering everywhere
   Her secret meaning in her deeds,      10
   And finding that of fifty seeds
She often brings but one to bear;

I falter where I firmly trod,
   And falling with my weight of cares
   Upon the great world's altar-stairs
That slope thro' darkness up to God;        15

I stretch lame hands of faith, and grope,
   And gather dust and chaff, and call
   To what I feel is Lord of all,
And faintly trust the larger hope.        20

### LVI

'So careful of the type?' but no.
   From scarped cliff and quarried stone
   She cries, 'A thousand types are gone:
I care for nothing, all shall go.

Thou makest thine appeal to me:        5
   I bring to life, I bring to death:
   The spirit does but mean the breath:
I know no more.' And he, shall he,

Man, her last work, who seemed so fair,
   Such splendid purpose in his eyes,
   Who rolled the psalm to wintry skies,        10
Who built him fanes of fruitless prayer,

Who trusted God was love indeed
   And love Creation's final law –
   Tho' Nature, red in tooth and claw        15
With ravine, shrieked against his creed –

Who loved, who suffered countless ills,
   Who battled for the True, the Just,
   Be blown about the desert dust,
Or sealed within the iron hills?        20

No more? A monster then, a dream,
   A discord. Dragons of the prime,
   That tare each other in their slime,
Were mellow music matched with him.

O life as futile, then, as frail!        25
   O for thy voice to soothe and bless!
   What hope of answer, or redress?
Behind the veil, behind the veil.

### LVII

Peace, come away: the song of woe
   Is after all an earthly song:

Peace, come away: we do him wrong
To sing so wildly: let us go.

Come, let us go, your cheeks are pale,                                    5
   But half my life I leave behind;
   Methinks my friend is richly shrined,
But I shall pass; my work will fail.[4]

Yet in these ears till hearing dies,
   One set slow bell will seem to toll                           10
   The passing of the sweetest soul
That ever looked with human eyes.

I hear it now, and o'er and o'er,
   Eternal greetings to the dead;
   And 'Ave, Ave, Ave,' said,                                     15
'Adieu, adieu' for evermore!

### LXXXVI

Sweet after showers, ambrosial air,
   That rollest from the gorgeous gloom
   Of evening over brake and bloom
And meadow, slowly breathing bare

The round of space, and rapt below                                        5
   Thro' all the dewy-tasselled wood,
   And shadowing down the horned flood
In ripples, fan my brows and blow

The fever from my cheek, and sigh
   The full new life that feeds thy breath                        10
   Throughout my frame, till Doubt and Death,
Ill brethren, let the fancy fly

From belt to belt of crimson seas
   On leagues of odour streaming far,
   To where in yonder orient star                                 15
A hundred spirits whisper 'Peace.'

### XCII

If any vision should reveal
   Thy likeness, I might count it vain
   As but the canker of the brain;
Yea, though it spake and made appeal

To chances where our lots were cast                                       5
   Together in the days behind,

---

[4] 'The poet speaks of these poems. Methinks I have built a rich shrine to my friend, but it will not last' (T.).

I might but say, I hear a wind
Of memory murmuring the past.

Yea, tho' it spake and bared to view
   A fact within the coming year;            10
   And tho' the months, revolving near,
Should prove the phantom-warning true,

They might not seem thy prophecies,
   But spiritual presentiments,
   And such refraction of events             15
As often rises ere they rise.

### XCIII

I shall not see thee. Dare I say
   No spirit ever brake the band
   That stays him from the native land
Where first he walked when claspt in clay?

No visual shade of some one lost,          5
   But he, the Spirit himself, may come
   Where all the nerve of sense is numb;
Spirit to Spirit, Ghost to Ghost.

O, therefore from thy sightless range
   With gods in unconjectured bliss,          10
   O, from the distance of the abyss
Of tenfold-complicated change,

Descend, and touch, and enter; hear
   The wish too strong for words to name;
   That in this blindness of the frame        15
My Ghost may feel that thine is near.

### XCIV

How pure at heart and sound in head,
   With what divine affections bold
   Should be the man whose thought would hold
An hour's communion with the dead.

In vain shalt thou, or any, call          5
   The spirits from their golden day,
   Except, like them, thou too canst say,
My spirit is at peace with all.

They haunt the silence of the breast,
   Imaginations calm and fair,          10
   The memory like a cloudless air,
The conscience as a sea at rest:

But when the heart is full of din,
   And doubt beside the portal waits,
   They can but listen at the gates,       15
And hear the household jar within.

### CVIII

I will not shut me from my kind,
   And, lest I stiffen into stone,
   I will not eat my heart alone,
Nor feed with sighs a passing wind:

What profit lies in barren faith,       5
   And vacant yearning, tho' with might
   To scale the heaven's highest height,
Or dive below the wells of Death?

What find I in the highest place,
   But mine own phantom chanting hymns?      10
   And on the depths of death there swims
The reflex of a human face.

I'll rather take what fruit may be
   Of sorrow under human skies:
   'Tis held that sorrow makes us wise,      15
Whatever wisdom sleep with thee.

### CXIX

Doors, where my heart was used to beat
   So quickly, not as one that weeps
   I come once more; the city sleeps;
I smell the meadow in the street;

I hear a chirp of birds; I see      5
   Betwixt the black fronts long-withdrawn
   A light-blue lane of early dawn,
And think of early days and thee,

And bless thee, for thy lips are bland,
   And bright the friendship of thine eye;      10
   And in my thoughts with scarce a sigh
I take the pressure of thine hand.

### CXXIX

Dear friend, far off, my lost desire,
   So far, so near in woe and weal;
   O loved the most, when most I feel
There is a lower and a higher;

Known and unknown; human, divine!     5
  Sweet human hand and lips and eye;
  Dear heavenly friend that canst not die,
Mine, mine, for ever, ever mine!

Strange friend, past, present, and to be,
  Loved deeplier, darklier understood;     10
  Behold I dream a dream of good,
And mingle all the world with thee.

### CXXX

Thy voice is on the rolling air;
  I hear thee where the waters run;
  Thou standest in the rising sun,
And in the setting thou art fair.

What art thou then? I cannot guess;     5
  But tho' I seem in star and flower
  To feel thee, some diffusive power,
I do not therefore love thee less:

My love involves the love before;
  My love is vaster passion now;     10
  Tho' mixed with God and Nature thou,
I seem to love thee more and more.

Far off thou art, but ever night;
  I have thee still, and I rejoice;
  I prosper, circled with thy voice;     15
I shall not lose thee though I die.

# The Charge of the Light Brigade

### I

Half a league, half a league,
  Half a league onward,
All in the valley of Death
  Rode the six hundred.
'Forward, the Light Brigade!     5
Charge for the guns!' he said:
Into the valley of Death
  Rode the six hundred.

### II

'Forward, the Light Brigade!'
Was there a man dismayed?     10
Not tho' the soldier knew

Some one had blundered:
Their's not to make reply,
Their's not to reason why,
Their's but to do and die:                                    15
Into the valley of Death
    Rode the six hundred.


### III

Cannon to right of them,
Cannon to left of them,
Cannon in front of them                                       20
    Volleyed and thundered;
Stormed at with shot and shell,
Boldly they rode and well,
Into the jaws of Death,
Into the mouth of Hell                                        25
    Rode the six hundred.


### IV

Flashed all their sabres bare,
Flashed as they turned in air
Sabring the gunners there,
Charging an army, while                                       30
    All the world wondered:
Plunged in the battery-smoke
Right thro' the line they broke;
Cossack and Russian
Reeled from the sabre-stroke                                  35
    Shattered and sundered.
Then they rode back, but not
    Not the six hundred.


### V

Cannon to right of them,
Cannon to left of them,                                       40
Cannon behind them
    Volleyed and thundered;
Stormed at with shot and shell,
While horse and hero fell,
They that had fought so well                                  45
Came thro' the jaws of Death,
Back from the mouth of Hell,
All that was left of them,
    Left of six hundred.


### VI

When can their glory fade?                                    50
O the wild charge they made!

All the world wondered.
Honour the charge they made!
Honour the Light Brigade,
   Noble six hundred!                                               55

# From: Maud

### I
### 1

I hate the dreadful hollow behind the little wood,
Its lips in the field above are dabbled with blood-red heath,
The red-ribbed ledges drip with a silent horror of blood,
And Echo there, whatever is asked her, answers 'Death.'

### 2

For there in the ghastly pit long since a body was found,            5
His who had given me life – O father! O God! was it well? –
Mangled, and flattened, and crushed, and dinted into the ground:
There yet lies the rock that fell with him when he fell.

### 3

Did he fling himself down? who knows? for a vast speculation had failed,
And ever he muttered and maddened, and ever wanned with despair,    10
And out he walked when the wind like a broken worldling wailed,
And the flying gold of the ruined woodlands drove thro' the air.

### 4

I remember the time, for the roots of my hair were stirred
By a shuffled step, by a dead weight trailed, by a whispered fright,
And my pulses closed their gates with a shock on my heart as I heard   15
The shrill-edged shriek of a mother divide the shuddering night.

### 5

Villainy somewhere! whose? One says, we are villains all.
Not he: his honest fame should at least by me be maintained:
But that old man, now lord of the broad estate and the Hall,
Dropt off gorged from a scheme that had left us flaccid and drained.   20

### 6

Why do they prate of the blessings of Peace? we have made them a curse,
Pickpockets, each hand lusting for all that is not its own;
And lust of gain, in the spirit of Cain, is it better or worse
Than the heart of the citizen hissing in war on his own hearthstone?

### 7

But these are the days of advance, the works of the men of mind,      25
When who but a fool would have faith in a tradesman's ware or his word?

Is it peace or war? Civil war, as I think, and that of a kind
The viler, as underhand, not openly bearing the sword.

### 8

Sooner or later I too may passively take the print
Of the golden age – why not? I have neither hope nor trust;                    30
May make my heart as a millstone, set my face as a flint,
Cheat and be cheated, and die: who knows? we are ashes and dust.

### 9

Peace sitting under her olive, and slurring the days gone by,
When the poor are hovelled and hustled together, each sex, like swine,
When only the ledger lives, and when only not all men lie;                     35
Peace in her vineyard – yes! – but a company forges the wine.

### 10

And the vitriol madness flushes up in the ruffian's head,
Till the filthy by-lane rings to the yell of the trampled wife,
And chalk and alum and plaster are sold to the poor for bread,
And the spirit of murder works in the very means of life,                      40

### 11

And Sleep must lie down armed, for the villainous centre-bits
Grind on the wakeful ear in the hush of the moonless nights,
While another is cheating the sick of a few last gasps, as he sits
To pestle a poisoned poison behind his crimson lights.

### 12

When a Mammonite mother kills her babe for a burial fee,                       45
And Timour-Mammon grins on a pile of children's bones,
Is it peace or war? better, war! loud war by land and by sea,
War with a thousand battles, and shaking a hundred thrones.

### 13

For I trust if an enemy's fleet came yonder round by the hill,
And the rushing battle-bolt sang from the three-decker out of the foam,        50
That the smoothfaced snubnosed rogue would leap from his counter and till,
And strike, if he could, were it but with his cheating yardwand, home. –

### 14

What! am I raging alone as my father raged in his mood?
Must *I* too creep to the hollow and dash myself down and die
Rather than hold by the law that I made, nevermore to brood                    55
On a horror of shattered limbs and a wretched swindler's lie?

### 15

Would there be sorrow for *me*? there was *love* in the passionate shriek,
Love for the silent thing that had made false haste to the grave –
Wrapt in a cloak, as I saw him, and thought he would rise and speak
And rave at the lie and the liar, ah God, as he used to rave.                    60

### 16

I am sick of the Hall and the hill, I am sick of the moor and the main.
Why should I stay? can a sweeter chance ever come to me here?
O, having the nerves of motion as well as the nerves of pain,
Were it not wise if I fled from the place and the pit and the fear?

### 17

There are workmen up at the Hall: they are coming back from abroad;     65
The dark old place will be gilt by the touch of a millionaire:
I have heard, I know not whence, of the singular beauty of Maud;
I played with the girl when a child; she promised then to be fair.

### 18

Maud with her venturous climbings and tumbles and childish escapes,
Maud the delight of the village, the ringing joy of the Hall,           70
Maud with her sweet purse-mouth when my father dangled the grapes,
Maud the beloved of my mother, the moon-faced darling of all, –

### 19

What is she now? My dreams are bad. She may bring me a curse.
No, there is fatter game on the moor; she will let me alone.
Thanks, for the fiend best knows whether woman or man be the worse.     75
I will bury myself in myself, and the Devil may pipe to his own.

### XXII
#### 1

Come into the garden, Maud,
  For the black bat, night, has flown,
Come into the garden, Maud,
  I am here at the gate alone;
And the woodbine spices are wafted abroad,          5
  And the musk of the rose is blown.

#### 2

For a breeze of morning moves,
  And the planet of Love is on high,
Beginning to faint in the light that she loves
  On a bed of daffodil sky,                          10

To faint in the light of the sun she loves,
To faint in his light, and to die.


### 3

All night have the roses heard
   The flute, violin, bassoon;
All night has the casement jessamine stirred         15
   To the dancers dancing in tune;
Till a silence fell with the waking bird,
   And a hush with the setting moon.


### 4

I said to the lily, 'There is but one
   With whom she has heart to be gay.         20
When will the dancers leave her alone?
   She is weary of dance and play.'
Now half to the setting moon are gone,
   And half to the rising day;
Low on the sand and loud on the stone         25
   The last wheel echoes away.


### 5

I said to the rose, 'The brief night goes
   In babble and revel and wine.
O young lord-lover, what sighs are those,
   For one that will never be thine?         30
But mine, but mine,' so I sware to the rose,
'For ever and ever, mine.'


### 6

And the soul of the rose went into my blood,
   As the music clashed in the hall;
And long by the garden lake I stood,         35
   For I heard your rivulet fall
From the lake to the meadow and on to the wood,
   Our wood, that is dearer than all;


### 7

From the meadow your walks have left so sweet
   That whenever a March-wind sighs         40
He sets the jewel-print of your feet
   In violets blue as your eyes,
To the woody hollows in which we meet
   And the valleys of Paradise.


### 8

The slender acacia would not shake         45
   One long milk-bloom on the tree;

The white lake-blossom fell into the lake
    As the pimpernel dozed on the lea;
But the rose was awake all night for your sake,
    Knowing your promise to me;          50
The lilies and roses were all awake,
    They sighed for the dawn and thee.

### 9

Queen rose of the rosebud garden of girls,
    Come hither, the dances are done,
In gloss of satin and glimmer of pearls,          55
    Queen lily and rose in one;
Shine out, little head, sunning over with curls,
    To the flowers, and be their sun.

### 10

There has fallen a splendid tear
    From the passion-flower at the gate.          60
She is coming, my dove, my dear;
    She is coming, my life, my fate;
The red rose cries, 'She is near, she is near;'
    And the white rose weeps, 'She is late;'
The larkspur listens, 'I hear, I hear;'          65
    And the lily whispers, 'I wait.'

### 11

She is coming, my own, my sweet;
    Were it ever so airy a tread,
My heart would hear her and beat,
    Were it earth in an earthy bed;          70
My dust would hear her and beat,
    Had I lain for a century dead;
Would start and tremble under her feet,
    And blossom in purple and red.

## Crossing the Bar

Sunset and evening star,
    And one clear call for me!
And may there be no moaning of the bar,
    When I put out to sea,

But such a tide as moving seems asleep,          5
    Too full for sound and foam,
When that which drew from out the boundless deep
    Turns again home.

Twilight and evening bell,
   And after that the dark!
And may there be no sadness of farewell,
   When I embark;

For tho' from out our bourne of Time and Place
   The flood may bear me far,
I hope to see my Pilot face to face
   When I have crost the bar.

# Robert Browning
# (1812–1889)

## My Last Duchess

*Ferrara*

That's my last Duchess painted on the wall,
Looking as if she were alive; I call
That piece a wonder, now: Fra Pandolf's hands
Worked busily a day, and there she stands.
Will't please you sit and look at her? I said          5
'Fra Pandolf' by design, for never read
Strangers like you that pictured countenance,
The depth and passion of its earnest glance,
But to myself they turned (since none puts by
The curtain I have drawn for you, but I)              10
And seemed as they would ask me, if they durst,
How such a glance came there; so not the first
Are you to turn and ask thus. Sir, 'twas not
Her husband's presence only, called that spot
Of joy into the Duchess' cheek: perhaps             15
Fra Pandolf chanced to say 'Her mantle laps
Over my lady's wrist too much,' or 'Paint
Must never hope to reproduce the faint
Half-flush that dies along her throat'; such stuff
Was courtesy, she thought, and cause enough          20
For calling up that spot of joy. She had
A heart . . how shall I say? . . too soon made glad,
Too easily impressed; she liked whate'er
She looked on, and her looks went everywhere.
Sir, 'twas all one! My favour at her breast,          25
The dropping of the daylight in the West,
The bough of cherries some officious fool
Broke in the orchard for her, the white mule
She rode with round the terrace – all and each
Would draw from her alike the forward speech,        30
Or blush, at least. She thanked men, – good; but thanked
Somehow . . . I know not how . . . as if she ranked
My gift of a nine hundred years old name
With anybody's gift. Who'd stoop to blame

This sort of trifling? Even had you skill                    35
In speech – (which I have not) – to make your will
Quite clear to such an one, and say, 'Just this
Or that in you disgusts me; here you miss,
Or there exceed the mark' – and if she let
Herself be lessoned so, nor plainly set                      40
Her wits to yours, forsooth, and made excuse,
– E'en then would be some stooping; and I chuse
Never to stoop. Oh, Sir, she smiled, no doubt,
Whene'er I passed her; but who passed without
Much the same smile? This grew; I gave commands;            45
Then all smiles stopped together. There she stands
As if alive. Will't please you rise? We'll meet
The company below then. I repeat,
The Count your Master's known munificence
Is ample warrant that no just pretence                       50
Of mine for dowry will be disallowed;
Though his fair daughter's self, as I avowed
At starting, is my object. Nay, we'll go
Together down, Sir! Notice Neptune, tho',
Taming a sea-horse, thought a rarity,                        55
Which Claus of Innsbruck cast in bronze for me.

# The Lost Leader

### I
Just for a handful of silver he left us,
    Just for a ribband to stick in his coat –
Got the one gift of which fortune bereft us,
    Lost all the others she lets us devote;
They, with the gold to give, doled him out silver,          5
    So much was their's who so little allowed:
How all our copper had gone for his service!
    Rags – were they purple, his heart had been proud!
We that had loved him so, followed him, honoured him,
    Lived in his mild and magnificent eye,                 10
Learned his great language, caught his clear accents,
    Made him our pattern to live and to die!
Shakespeare was of us, Milton was for us,
    Burns, Shelley, were with us, – they watch from their graves!
He alone breaks from the van and the freemen,               15
    – He alone sinks to the rear and the slaves!

### II
We shall march prospering, – not thro' his presence;
    Songs may excite us, – not from his lyre;
Deeds will be done, – while he boasts his quiescence,

Still bidding crouch whom the rest bade aspire:                                    20
Blot out his name, then, – record one lost soul more,
   One task unaccepted, one footpath untrod,
One more devils'-triumph and sorrow for angels,
   One wrong more to man, one more insult to God!
Life's night begins: let him never come back to us!                               25
   There would be doubt, hesitation and pain,
Forced praise on our part – the glimmer of twilight,
   Never glad confident morning again!
Best fight on well, for we taught him, – come gallantly,
   Strike our face hard ere we shatter his own;                         30
Then let him get the new knowledge and wait us,
   Pardoned in Heaven, the first by the throne!


# Soliloquy of the Spanish Cloister

### I

GR-R-R – there go, my heart's abhorrence!
   Water your damned flower-pots, do!
If hate killed men, Brother Lawrence,
   God's blood, would not mine kill you!
What? your myrtle-bush wants trimming?                                            5
   Oh, that rose has prior claims –
Needs its leaden vase filled brimming?
   Hell dry you up with its flames!


### II

At the meal we sit together:
   *Salve tibi!* I must hear                                           10
Wise talk of the kind of weather,
   Sort of season, time of year:
*Not a plenteous cork-crop: scarcely*
   *Dare we hope oak-galls, I doubt:*
*What's the Latin name for 'parsley'?*                                            15
   What's the Greek name for Swine's Snout?


### III

Phew! We'll have our platter burnished,
   Laid with care on our own shelf !
With a fire-new spoon we're furnished,
   And a goblet for ourself,                                            20
Rinsed like something sacrificial
   Ere 'tis fit to touch our chaps –
Marked with L. for our initial!
   (He-he! There his lily snaps!)

### IV

*Saint*, forsooth! While brown Dolores                    25
 Squats outside the Convent bank
With Sanchicha, telling stories,
 Steeping tresses in the tank,
Blue-black, lustrous, thick like horsehairs,
 – Can't I see his dead eye grow,                    30
Bright as 'twere a Barbary corsair's?
 That is, if he'd let it show!

### V

When he finishes refection,
 Knife and fork across he lays
Never, to my recollection,                              35
 As do I, in Jesu's praise.
I, the Trinity illustrate,
 Drinking watered orange-pulp;
In three sips the Arian frustrate;
 While he drains his at one gulp!                    40

### VI

Oh, those melons? If he's able
 We're to have a feast; so nice!
One goes to the Abbot's table,
 All of us get each a slice.
How go on your flowers? None double?                    45
 Not one fruit-sort can you spy?
Strange! – And I, too, at such trouble,
 Keep 'em close-nipped on the sly!

### VII

There's a great text in Galatians,
 Once you trip on it, entails                        50
Twenty-nine distinct damnations,
 One sure, if another fails:
If I trip him just a-dying,
 Sure of Heaven as sure can be,
Spin him round and send him flying                      55
 Off to hell a Manichee?

### VIII

Or, my scrofulous French novel
 On grey paper with blunt type!
Simply glance at it, you grovel
 Hand and foot in Belial's gripe.                    60
If I double down its pages
 At the woeful sixteenth print,

When he gathers his greengages,
    Ope a sieve and slip it in't?

IX

Or, the Devil! – one might venture         65
    Pledge one's soul yet slily leave
Such a flaw in the indenture
    As he'd miss till, past retrieve,
Blasted lay that rose-acacia
    We're so proud of ! *Hy, Zy, Hine* . . .    70
St, there's Vespers! *Plena gratiâ*
    *Ave, Virgo!* Gr-r-r – you swine!

# Porphyria's Lover

The rain set early in tonight,
    The sullen wind was soon awake,
It tore the elm-tops down for spite,
    And did its worst to vex the lake,
    I listened with heart fit to break,    5
When glided in Porphyria; straight
    She shut the cold out and the storm,
And kneeled and made the cheerless grate
    Blaze up, and all the cottage warm;
    Which done, she rose, and from her form    10
Withdrew the dripping cloak and shawl,
    And laid her soiled gloves by, untied
Her hat and let the damp hair fall,
    And, last, she sat down by my side
    And called me. When no voice replied,    15
She put my arm about her waist,
    And made her smooth white shoulder bare,
And all her yellow hair displaced,
    And, stooping, made my cheek lie there,
    And spread o'er all her yellow hair,    20
Murmuring how she loved me; she
    Too weak, for all her heart's endeavour,
To set its struggling passion free
    From pride, and vainer ties dissever,
    And give herself to me for ever:    25
But passion sometimes would prevail,
    Nor could tonight's gay feast restrain
A sudden thought of one so pale
    For love of her, and all in vain;
    And she was come through wind and rain.    30
Be sure I looked up at her eyes
    Proud, very proud; at last I knew

Porphyria worshipped me; surprise
   Made my heart swell, and still it grew
   While I debated what to do.                                        35
That moment she was mine, mine, fair,
   Perfectly pure and good: I found
A thing to do, and all her hair
   In one long yellow string I wound
   Three times her little throat around,                              40
And strangled her. No pain felt she;
   I am quite sure she felt no pain.
As a shut bud that holds a bee
   I warily oped her lids; again
   Laughed the blue eyes without a stain.                             45
And I untightened next the tress
   About her neck; her cheek once more
Blushed bright beneath my burning kiss:
   I propped her head up as before,
   Only, this time my shoulder bore                                   50
Her head, which droops upon it still:
   The smiling rosy little head,
So glad it has its utmost will,
   That all it scorned at once is fled,
   And I, its love, am gained instead!                               55
Porphyria's love: she guessed not how
   Her darling one wish would be heard.
And thus we sit together now,
   And all night long we have not stirred,
   And yet God has not said a word!                                   60

## Home-Thoughts, from Abroad

### I

Oh, to be in England
Now that April's there,
And whoever wakes in England
Sees, some morning, unaware,
That the lowest boughs and the brush-wood sheaf                          5
Round the elm-tree bole are in tiny leaf,
While the chaffinch sings on the orchard bough
In England – now!

### II

And after April, when May follows,
And the whitethroat builds, and all the swallows –                       10
Hark! where my blossomed pear-tree in the hedge
Leans to the field and scatters on the clover
Blossoms and dewdrops – at the bent spray's edge –

That's the wise thrush; he sings each song twice over,
Lest you should think he never could recapture                    15
The first fine careless rapture!
And though the fields look rough with hoary dew,
All will be gay when noontide wakes anew
The buttercups, the little children's dower,
 – Far brighter than this gaudy melon-flower!                     20

# The Bishop Orders His Tomb
## at Saint Praxed's Church

*Rome, 15 —*

Vanity, saith the preacher, vanity!
Draw round my bed: is Anselm keeping back?
Nephews – sons mine . . . ah God, I know not! Well –
She, men would have to be your mother once,
Old Gandolf envied me, so fair she was!                           5
What's done is done, and she is dead beside,
Dead long ago, and I am Bishop since,
And as she died so must we die ourselves,
And thence ye may perceive the world's a dream.
Life, how and what is it? As here I lie                           10
In this state-chamber, dying by degrees,
Hours and long hours in the dead night, I ask
'Do I live, am I dead?' Peace, peace seems all:
St Praxed's ever was the church for peace;
And so, about this tomb of mine. I fought                         15
With tooth and nail to save my niche, ye know:
 – Old Gandolf cozened me, despite my care;
Shrewd was that snatch from out the corner South
He graced his carrion with, God curse the same!
Yet still my niche is not so cramped but thence                   20
One sees the pulpit o' the epistle-side,
And somewhat of the choir, those silent seats,
And up into the aery dome where live
The angels, and a sunbeam's sure to lurk:
And I shall fill my slab of basalt there,                         25
And 'neath my tabernacle take my rest
With those nine columns round me, two and two,
The odd one at my feet where Anselm stands:
Peach-blossom marble all, the rare, the ripe
As fresh-poured red wine of a mighty pulse.                       30
 – Old Gandolf with his paltry onion-stone,
Put me where I may look at him! True peach,
Rosy and flawless: how I earned the prize!
Draw close: that conflagration of my church

– What then? So much was saved if aught were missed!          35
My sons, ye would not be my death? Go dig
The white-grape vineyard where the oil-press stood,
Drop water gently till the surface sinks,
And if ye find . . . Ah, God, I know not, I! . . .
Bedded in store of rotten figleaves soft,                    40
And corded up in a tight olive-frail,
Some lump, ah God, of *lapis lazuli*,
Big as a Jew's head cut off at the nape,
Blue as a vein o'er the Madonna's breast . . .
Sons, all have I bequeathed you, villas, all,                45
That brave Frascati villa with its bath,
So let the blue lump poise between my knees,
Like God the Father's globe on both his hands
Ye worship in the Jesu Church so gay,
For Gandolf shall not choose but see and burst!             50
Swift as a weaver's shuttle fleet our years:
Man goeth to the grave, and where is he?
Did I say basalt for my slab, sons? Black –
'Twas ever antique-black I meant! How else
Shall ye contrast my frieze to come beneath?                55
The bas-relief in bronze ye promised me,
Those Pans and Nymphs ye wot of, and perchance
Some tripod, thyrsus, with a vase or so,
The Saviour at his sermon on the mount,
St Praxed in a glory, and one Pan                            60
Ready to twitch the Nymph's last garment off,
And Moses with the tables . . . but I know
Ye mark me not! What do they whisper thee,
Child of my bowels, Anselm? Ah, ye hope
To revel down my villas while I gasp                         65
Bricked o'er with beggar's mouldy travertine
Which Gandolf from his tomb-top chuckles at!
Nay, boys, ye love me – all of jasper, then!
'Tis jasper ye stand pledged to, lest I grieve
My bath must needs be left behind, alas!                     70
One block, pure green as a pistachio-nut,
There's plenty jasper somewhere in the world –
And have I not St Praxed's ear to pray
Horses for ye, and brown Greek manuscripts,
And mistresses with great smooth marbly limbs?              75
 – That's if ye carve my epitaph aright,
Choice Latin, picked phrase, Tully's every word,
No gaudy ware like Gandolf's second line –
Tully, my masters? Ulpian serves his need!
And then how I shall lie through centuries,                  80

And hear the blessed mutter of the mass,
And see God made and eaten all day long,
And feel the steady candle-flame, and taste
Good strong thick stupifying incense-smoke!
For as I lie here, hours of the dead night,          85
Dying in state and by such slow degrees,
I fold my arms as if they clasped a crook,
And stretch my feet forth straight as stone can point,
And let the bedclothes for a mortcloth drop
Into great laps and folds of sculptor's-work:         90
And as yon tapers dwindle, and strange thoughts
Grow, with a certain humming in my ears,
About the life before this life I lived,
And this life too, Popes, Cardinals and Priests,
St Praxed at his sermon on the mount,         95
Your tall pale mother with her talking eyes,
And new-found agate urns as fresh as day,
And marble's language, Latin pure, discreet,
– Aha, ELUCESCEBAT quoth our friend?
No Tully, said I, Ulpian at the best!         100
Evil and brief hath been my pilgrimage,
All *lapis*, all, sons! Else I give the Pope
My villas: will ye ever eat my heart?
Ever your eyes were as a lizard's quick,
They glitter like your mother's for my soul,         105
Or ye would heighten my impoverished frieze,
Piece out its starved design, and fill my vase
With grapes, and add a vizor and a Term,
And to the tripod ye would tie a lynx
That in his struggle throws the thyrsus down,         110
To comfort me on my entablature
Whereon I am to lie till I must ask
'Do I live, am I dead?' There, leave me, there!
For ye have stabbed me with ingratitude
To death – ye wish it – God, ye wish it! Stone –         115
Gritstone, a-crumble! Clammy squares which sweat
As if the corpse they keep were oozing through –
And no more *lapis* to delight the world!
Well go! I bless ye. Fewer tapers there,
But in a row: and, going, turn your backs         120
– Ay, like departing altar-ministrants,
And leave me in my church, the church for peace,
That I may watch at leisure if he leers –
Old Gandolf, at me, from his onion-stone,
As still he envied me, so fair she was!         125

# Meeting at Night

### I

The grey sea and the long black land;
And the yellow half-moon large and low;
And the startled little waves that leap
In fiery ringlets from their sleep,
As I gain the cove with pushing prow,                    5
And quench its speed in the slushy sand.

### II

Then a mile of warm sea-scented beach;
Three fields to cross till a farm appears;
A tap at the pane, the quick sharp scratch
And blue spurt of a lighted match,                       10
And a voice less loud, thro' its joys and fears,
Than the two hearts beating each to each!

# Parting at Morning

Round the cape of a sudden came the sea,
And the sun looked over the mountain's rim –
And straight was a path of gold for him,
And the need of a world of men for me.

# Love Among the Ruins

### 1

Where the quiet-coloured end of evening smiles,
    Miles and miles
On the solitary pastures where our sheep
    Half-asleep
Tinkle homeward thro' the twilight, stray or stop        5
    As they crop –

### 2

Was the site once of a city great and gay,
    (So they say)
Of our country's very capital, its prince
    Ages since                                           10
Held his court in, gathered councils, wielding far
    Peace or war.

3

Now – the country does not even boast a tree,
   As you see,
To distinguish slopes of verdure, certain rills           15
   From the hills
Intersect and give a name to (else they run
   Into one),

4

Where the domed and daring palace shot its spires
   Up like fires           20
O'er the hundred-gated circuit of a wall
   Bounding all,
Made of marble, men might march on nor be pressed,
   Twelve abreast.

5

And such plenty and perfection, see, of grass          25
   Never was!
Such a carpet as, this summer-time, o'erspreads
   And embeds
Every vestige of the city, guessed alone,
   Stock or stone –          30

6

Where a multitude of men breathed joy and woe
   Long ago;
Lust of glory pricked their hearts up, dread of shame
   Struck them tame;
And that glory and that shame alike, the gold        35
   Bought and sold.

7

Now, – the single little turret that remains
   On the plains,
By the caper over-rooted, by the gourd
   Overscored,          40
While the patching houseleek's head of blossom winks
   Through the chinks –

8

Marks the basement whence a tower in ancient time
   Sprang sublime,
And a burning ring all round, the chariots traced      45
   As they raced,

And the monarch and his minions and his dames
  Viewed the games.


9

And I know, while thus the quiet-coloured eve
  Smiles to leave                                            50
to their folding, all our many-tinkling fleece
  In such peace,
And the slopes and rills in undistinguished grey
  Melt away –


10

That a girl with eager eyes and yellow hair              55
  Waits me there
In the turret whence the charioteers caught soul
  For the goal,
When the king looked, where she looks now, breathless, dumb
  Till I come.                                               60


11

But he looked upon the city, every side,
  Far and wide,
All the mountains topped with temples, all the glades'
  Colonnades,
All the causeys, bridges, aqueducts, – and then,       65
  All the men!


12

When I do come, she will speak not, she will stand,
  Either hand
On my shoulder, give her eyes the first embrace
  Of my face,                                                70
Ere we rush, ere we extinguish sight and speech
  Each on each.


13

In one year they sent a million fighters forth
  South and North,
And they built their gods a brazen pillar high         75
  As the sky,
Yet reserved a thousand chariots in full force –
  Gold, of course.


14

Oh, heart! oh, blood that freezes, blood that burns!
  Earth's returns                                            80
For whole centuries of folly, noise and sin!
  Shut them in,

With their triumphs and their glories and the rest!
Love is best.


# Fra Lippo Lippi

I am poor brother Lippo, by your leave!
You need not clap your torches to my face.
Zooks, what's to blame? you think you see a monk!
What, it's past midnight, and you go the rounds,
And here you catch me at an alley's end                                     5
Where sportive ladies leave their doors ajar.
The Carmine's my cloister: hunt it up,
Do, – harry out, if you must show your zeal,
Whatever rat, there, haps on his wrong hole,
And nip each softling of a wee white mouse,                                 10
Weke, weke, that's crept to keep him company!
Aha, you know your betters! Then, you'll take
Your hand away that's fiddling on my throat,
And please to know me likewise. Who am I?
Why, one, sir, who is lodging with a friend                                 15
Three streets off – he's a certain . . . how d'ye call?
Master – a . . . Cosimo of the Medici,
I' the house that caps the corner. Boh! you were best!
Remember and tell me, the day you're hanged,
How you affected such a gullet's-gripe!                                     20
But you, sir, it concerns you that your knaves
Pick up a manner nor discredit you.
Zooks, are we pilchards, that they sweep the streets
And count fair prize what comes into their net?
He's Judas to a tittle, that man is!                                        25
Just such a face! why, sir, you make amends.
Lord, I'm not angry! Bid your hangdogs go
Drink out this quarter-florin to the health
Of the munificent House that harbours me
(And many more beside, lads! more beside!)                                  30
And all's come square again. I'd like his face –
His, elbowing on his comrade in the door
With the pike and lantern, – for the slave that holds
John Baptist's head a-dangle by the hair
With one hand ('Look you, now,' as who should say)                         35
And his weapon in the other, yet unwiped!
It's not your chance to have a bit of chalk,
A wood-coal or the like? or you should see!
Yes, I'm the painter, since you style me so.
What, brother Lippo's doings, up and down,                                  40
You know them and they take you? like enough!
I saw the proper twinkle in your eye –

'Tell you I liked your looks at very first.
Let's sit and set things straight now, hip to haunch.
Here's spring come, and the nights one makes up bands            45
To roam the town and sing out carnival,
And I've been three weeks shut within my mew,
A-painting for the great man, saints and saints
And saints again. I could not paint all night –
Ouf ! I leaned out of window for fresh air.                      50
There came a hurry of feet and little feet,
A sweep of lute-strings, laughs, and whiffs of song, –
*Flower o' the broom,*
*Take away love, and our earth is a tomb!*
*Flower o' the quince,*                                          55
*I let Lisa go, and what good's in life since?*
*Flower o' the thyme* – and so on. Round they went.
Scarce had they turned the corner when a titter
Like the skipping of rabbits by moonlight, – three slim shapes –
And a face that looked up . . . zooks, sir, flesh and blood,     60
That's all I'm made of! Into shreds it went,
Curtain and counterpane and coverlet,
All the bed-furniture – a dozen knots,
There was a ladder! down I let myself,
Hands and feet, scrambling somehow, and so dropped,              65
And after them. I came up with the fun
Hard by Saint Laurence, hail fellow, well met, –
*Flower o' the rose,*
*If I've been merry, what matter who knows?*
And so as I was stealing back again                              70
To get to bed and have a bit of sleep
Ere I rise up tomorrow and go work
On Jerome knocking at his poor old breast
With his great round stone to subdue the flesh,
You snap me of the sudden. Ah, I see!                            75
Though your eye twinkles still, you shake your head –
Mine's shaved, – a monk, you say – the sting's in that!
If Master Cosimo announced himself,
Mum's the word naturally; but a monk!
Come, what am I a beast for? tell us, now!                       80
I was a baby when my mother died
And father died and left me in the street.
I starved there, God knows how, a year or two
On fig-skins, melon-parings, rinds and shucks,
Refuse and rubbish. One fine frosty day,                         85
My stomach being empty as your hat,
The wind doubled me up and down I went.
Old Aunt Lapaccia trussed me with one hand,
(Its fellow was a stinger as I knew)
And so along the wall, over the bridge,                          90

By the straight cut to the convent. Six words, there,
While I stood munching my first bread that month:
'So, boy, you're minded,' quoth the good fat father
Wiping his own mouth, 'twas refection-time, –
'To quit this very miserable world?                                          95
Will you renounce'...the mouthful of bread? thought I;
By no means! Brief, they made a monk of me;
I did renounce the world, its pride and greed,
Palace, farm, villa, shop and banking-house,
Trash, such as these poor devils of Medici                                  100
Have given their hearts to – all at eight years old.
Well, sir, I found in time, you may be sure,
'Twas not for nothing – the good bellyful,
The warm serge and the rope that goes all round,
And day-long blessed idleness beside!                                       105
'Let's see what the urchin's fit for' – that came next.
Not overmuch their way, I must confess.
Such a to-do! they tried me with their books.
Lord, they'd have taught me Latin in pure waste!
*Flower o' the clove,*                                                      110
*All the Latin I construe is, 'amo' I love!*
But, mind you, when a boy starves in the streets
Eight years together, as my fortune was,
Watching folk's faces to know who will fling
The bit of half-stripped grape-bunch he desires,                           115
And who will curse or kick him for his pains –
Which gentleman processional and fine,
Holding a candle to the Sacrament,
Will wink and let him lift a plate and catch
The droppings of the wax to sell again,                                     120
Or holla for the Eight and have him whipped, –
How say I? – nay, which dog bites, which lets drop
His bone from the heap of offal in the street!
– The soul and sense of him grow sharp alike,
He learns the look of things, and none the less                            125
For admonitions from the hunger-pinch.
I had a store of such remarks, be sure,
Which, after I found leisure, turned to use:
I drew men's faces on my copy-books,
Scrawled them within the antiphonary's marge,                              130
Joined legs and arms to the long music-notes,
Found eyes and nose and chin for A.s and B.s,
And made a string of pictures of the world
Betwixt the ins and outs of verb and noun,
On the wall, the bench, the door. The monks looked black.                  135
'Nay,' quoth the Prior, 'turn him out, d'ye say?
In no wise. Lose a crow and catch a lark.
What if at last we get our man of parts,

We Carmelites, like those Camaldolese
And Preaching Friars, to do our church up fine          140
And put the front on it that ought to be!'
And hereupon he bade me daub away.
Thank you! my head being crammed, their walls a blank,
Never was such prompt disemburdening.
First, every sort of monk, the black and white,          145
I drew them, fat and lean: then, folk at church,
From good old gossips waiting to confess
Their cribs of barrel-droppings, candle-ends, –
To the breathless fellow at the altar-foot,
Fresh from his murder, safe and sitting there          150
With the little children round him in a row
Of admiration, half for his beard and half
For that white anger of his victim's son
Shaking a fist at him with one fierce arm,
Signing himself with the other because of Christ          155
(Whose sad face on the cross sees only this
After the passion of a thousand years)
Till some poor girl, her apron o'er her head
Which the intense eyes looked through, came at eve
On tip-toe, said a word, dropped in a loaf,          160
Her pair of earrings and a bunch of flowers
The brute took growling, prayed, and then was gone.
I painted all, then cried ''tis ask and have –
Choose, for more's ready!' – laid the ladder flat,
And showed my covered bit of cloister-wall.          165
The monks closed in a circle and praised loud
Till checked, (taught what to see and not to see,
Being simple bodies) 'that's the very man!
Look at the boy who stoops to pat the dog!
That woman's like the Prior's niece who comes          170
To care about his asthma: it's the life!'
But there my triumph's straw-fire flared and funked;
Their betters took their turn to see and say:
The Prior and the learned pulled a face
And stopped all that in no time. 'How? what's here?          175
Quite from the mark of painting, bless us all!
Faces, arms, legs and bodies like the true
As much as pea and pea! it's devil's-game!
Your business is not to catch men with show,
With homage to the perishable clay,          180
But lift them over it, ignore it all,
Make them forget there's such a thing as flesh.
Your business is to paint the souls of men –
Man's soul, and it's a fire, smoke . . .no, it's not. . .
It's vapour done up like a new-born babe –          185
(In that shape when you die it leaves your mouth)

It's… well, what matters talking, it's the soul!
Give us no more of body than shows soul!
Here's Giotto, with his Saint a-praising God,
That sets us praising, – why not stop with him?                        190
Why put all thoughts of praise out of our heads
With wonder at lines, colours, and what not?
Paint the soul, never mind the legs and arms!
Rub all out, try at it a second time.
Oh, that white smallish female with the breasts,                        195
She's just my niece… Herodias, I would say, –
Who went and danced and got men's heads cut off!
Have it all out!' Now, is this sense, I ask?
A fine way to paint soul, by painting body
So ill, the eye can't stop there, must go further                       200
And can't fare worse! Thus, yellow does for white
When what you put for yellow's simply black,
And any sort of meaning looks intense
When all beside itself means and looks nought.
Why can't a painter lift each foot in turn,                             205
Left foot and right foot, go a double step,
Make his flesh liker and his soul more like,
Both in their order? Take the prettiest face,
The Prior's niece… patron-saint – is it so pretty
You can't discover if it means hope, fear,                             210
Sorrow or joy? won't beauty go with these?
Suppose I've made her eyes all right and blue,
Can't I take breath and try to add life's flash,
And then add soul and heighten them threefold?
Or say there's beauty with no soul at all –                            215
(I never saw it – put the case the same –)
If you get simple beauty and nought else,
You get about the best thing God invents, –
That's somewhat. And you'll find the soul you have missed,
Within yourself, when you return Him thanks!                           220
'Rub all out!' well, well, there's my life, in short,
And so the thing has gone on ever since.
I'm grown a man no doubt, I've broken bounds –
You should not take a fellow eight years old
And make him swear to never kiss the girls –                           225
I'm my own master, paint now as I please –
Having a friend, you see, in the Corner-house!
Lord, it's fast holding by the rings in front –
Those great rings serve more purposes than just
To plant a flag in, or tie up a horse!                                 230
And yet the old schooling sticks, the old grave eyes
Are peeping o'er my shoulder as I work,
The heads shake still – 'It's Art's decline, my son!
You're not of the true painters, great and old:

Brother Angelico's the man, you'll find:                                235
Brother Lorenzo stands his single peer.
Fag on at flesh, you'll never make the third!'
*Flower o' the pine,*
*You keep your mistr... manners, and I'll stick to mine!*
I'm not the third, then: bless us, they must know!              240
Don't you think they're the likeliest to know,
They, with their Latin? so, I swallow my rage,
Clench my teeth, suck my lips in tight, and paint
To please them – sometimes do and sometimes don't,
For, doing most, there's pretty sure to come                    245
A turn – some warm eve finds me at my saints –
A laugh, a cry, the business of the world –
(*Flower o' the peach,*
*Death for us all, and his own life for each!*)
And my whole soul revolves, the cup runs o'er,                 250
The world and life's too big to pass for a dream,
And I do these wild things in sheer despite,
And play the fooleries you catch me at,
In pure rage! the old mill-horse, out at grass
After hard years, throws up his stiff heels so,                 255
Although the miller does not preach to him
The only good of grass is to make chaff.
What would men have? Do they like grass or no –
May they or mayn't they? all I want's the thing
Settled for ever one way: as it is,                             260
You tell too many lies and hurt yourself.
You don't like what you only like too much,
You do like what, if given you at your word,
You find abundantly detestable.
For me, I think I speak as I was taught;                        265
I always see the Garden and God there
A-making man's wife – and, my lesson learned,
The value and significance of flesh,
I can't unlearn ten minutes afterwards.
    You understand me: I'm a beast, I know.                     270
But see, now – why, I see as certainly
As that the morning-star's about to shine,
What will hap some day. We've a youngster here
Comes to our convent, studies what I do,
Slouches and stares and lets no atom drop –                    275
His name is Guidi – he'll not mind the monks –
They call him Hulking Tom, he lets them talk –
He picks my practice up – he'll paint apace,
I hope so – though I never live so long,
I know what's sure to follow. You be judge!                    280
You speak no Latin more than I, belike –
However, you're my man, you've seen the world

– The beauty and the wonder and the power,
The shapes of things, their colours, lights and shades,
Changes, surprises, – and God made it all!                              285
– For what? do you feel thankful, ay or no,
For this fair town's face, yonder river's line,
The mountain round it and the sky above,
Much more the figures of man, woman, child,
These are the frame to? What's it all about?                            290
To be passed o'er, despised? or dwelt upon,
Wondered at? oh, this last of course, you say.
But why not do as well as say, – paint these
Just as they are, careless what comes of it?
God's works – paint anyone, and count it crime                          295
To let a truth slip. Don't object, 'His works
Are here already; nature is complete:
Suppose you reproduce her – (which you can't)
There's no advantage! you must beat her, then.'
For, don't you mark? we're made so that we love                         300
First when we see them painted, things we have passed
Perhaps a hundred times nor cared to see;
And so they are better, painted – better to us,
Which is the same thing. Art was given for that –
God uses us to help each other so,                                      305
Lending our minds out. Have you noticed, now,
Your cullion's hanging face? A bit of chalk,
And trust me but you should, though! How much more,
If I drew higher things with the same truth!
That were to take the Prior's pulpit-place,                             310
Interpret God to all of you! oh, oh,
It makes me mad to see what men shall do
And we in our graves! This world's no blot for us,
Nor blank – it means intensely, and means good:
To find its meaning is my meat and drink.                               315
'Ay, but you don't so instigate to prayer'
Strikes in the Prior! 'when your meaning's plain
It does not say to folk – remember matins –
Or, mind you fast next Friday!' Why, for this
What need of art at all? A skull and bones,                             320
Two bits of stick nailed crosswise, or, what's best,
A bell to chime the hour with, does as well.
I painted a St Laurence six months since
At Prato, splashed the fresco in fine style.
'How looks my painting, now the scaffold's down?'                       325
I ask a brother: 'Hugely,' he returns –
'Already not one phiz of your three slaves
Who turn the Deacon off his toasted side,
But's scratched and prodded to our heart's content,
The pious people have so eased their own                                330

With coming to say prayers there in a rage.
We get on fast to see the bricks beneath.
Expect another job this time next year,
For pity and religion grow i' the crowd –
Your painting serves its purpose!' Hang the fools!                335
– That is – you'll not mistake an idle word
Spoke in a huff by a poor monk, Got wot,
Tasting the air this spicy night which turns
The unaccustomed head like Chianti wine!
Oh, the church knows! don't misreport me, now!                   340
It's natural a poor monk out of bounds
Should have his apt word to excuse himself:
And hearken how I plot to make amends.
I have bethought me: I shall paint a piece
. . . There's for you! Give me six months, then go, see            345
Something in Sant' Ambrogio's! (bless the nuns!
They want a cast of my office). I shall paint
God in the midst, Madonna and her babe,
Ringed by a bowery, flowery angel-brood,
Lilies and vestments and white faces, sweet                       350
As puff on puff of grated orris-root
When ladies crowd to Church at midsummer.
And then in the front, of course a saint or two –
Saint John, because he saves the Florentines,
Saint Ambrose, who puts down in black and white                  355
The convent's friends and gives them a long day,
And Job, I must have him there past mistake,
The man of Uz (and Us without the z,
Painters who need his patience). Well, all these
Secured at their devotions, up shall come                         360
Out of a corner when you least expect,
As one by a dark stair into a great light
Music and talking, who but Lippo! I! –
Mazed, motionless and moon-struck – I'm the man!
Back I shrink – what is this I see and hear?                      365
I, caught up with my monk's-things by mistake,
My old serge gown and rope that goes all round,
I, in this presence, this pure company!
Where's a hole, where's a corner for escape?
Then steps a sweet angelic slip of a thing                        370
Forward, puts out a soft palm – 'Not so fast!'
– Addresses the celestial presence, 'nay –
He made you and devised you, after all,
Though he's none of you! Could Saint John there, draw –
His camel-hair make up a painting-brush?                          375
We come to brother Lippo for all that,
*Iste perfecit opus!* So, all smile –

I shuffle sideways with my blushing face
Under the cover of a hundred wings
Thrown like a spread of kirtles when you're gay 380
And play hot cockles, all the doors being shut,
Till, wholly unexpected, in there pops
The hothead husband! Thus I scuttle off
To some safe bench behind, not letting go
The palm of her, the little lily thing 385
That spoke the good word for me in the nick,
Like the Prior's niece ... Saint Lucy, I would say.
And so all's saved for me, and for the church
A pretty picture gained. Go, six months hence!
Your hand, sir, and good bye: no lights, no lights! 390
The street's hushed, and I know my own way back –
Don't fear me! There's the grey beginning. Zooks!

# A Toccata of Galuppi's

### 1
Oh Galuppi, Baldassaro, this is very sad to find!
I can hardly misconceive you; it would prove me deaf and blind;
But although I take your meaning, 'tis with such a heavy mind!

### 2
Here you come with your old music, and here's all the good it brings.
What, they lived once thus at Venice where the merchants were the kings, 5
Where Saint Mark's is, where the Doges used to wed the sea with rings?

### 3
Ay, because the sea's the street there; and 'tis arched by ... what you call
... Shylock's bridge with houses on it, where they kept the carnival!
I was never out of England – it's as if I saw it all.

### 4
Did young people take their pleasure when the sea was warm in May? 10
Balls and masks begun at midnight, burning ever to midday,
When they made up fresh adventures for the morrow, do you say?

### 5
Was a lady such a lady, cheeks so round and lips so red, –
On her neck the small face buoyant, like a bell-flower on its bed,
O'er the breast's superb abundance where a man might base his head? 15

### 6
Well, (and it was graceful of them) they'd break talk off and afford
– She, to bite her mask's black velvet, he to finger on his sword,
While you sat and played Toccatas, stately at the clavichord?

### 7

What? Those lesser thirds so plaintive, sixths diminished, sigh on sigh,
Told them something? Those suspensions, those solutions – 'Must we die?'   20
Those commiserating sevenths – 'Life might last! we can but try!'

### 8

'Were you happy?' – 'Yes.' – 'And are you still as happy?' – 'Yes – And you?'
– 'Then, more kisses' – 'Did *I* stop them, when a million seemed so few?'
Hark – the dominant's persistence, till it must be answered to!

### 9

So an octave struck the answer. Oh, they praised you, I dare say!   25
'Brave Galuppi! that was music! good alike at grave and gay!
I can always leave off talking when I hear a master play.'

### 10

Then they left you for their pleasure: till in due time, one by one,
Some with lives that came to nothing, some with deeds as well undone,
Death stepped tacitly and took them where they never see the sun.   30

### 11

But when I sit down to reason, – think to take my stand nor swerve,
While I triumph o'er a secret wrung from nature's close reserve,
In you come with your cold music till I creep thro' every nerve.

### 12

Yes, you, like a ghostly cricket, creaking where a house was burned –
'Dust and ashes, dead and done with, Venice spent what Venice earned.   35
The soul, doubtless, is immortal – where a soul can be discerned.

### 13

'Yours for instance: you know physics, something of geology,
Mathematics are your pastime; souls shall rise in their degree;
Butterflies may dread extinction, – you'll not die, it cannot be!

### 14

'As for Venice and its people, merely born to bloom and drop,   40
Here on earth they bore their fruitage, mirth and folly were the crop.
What of soul was left, I wonder, when the kissing had to stop?

### 15

'Dust and ashes!' So you creak it, and I want the heart to scold.
Dear dead women, with such hair, too – what's become of all the gold
Used to hang and brush their bosoms? I feel chilly and grown old.   45

# 'Childe Roland to the Dark Tower Came'

## *(See Edgar's song in 'Lear')*

### 1

My first thought was, he lied in every word,
    That hoary cripple, with malicious eye
    Askance to watch the working of his lie
On mine, and mouth scarce able to afford
Suppression of the glee that pursed and scored       5
    Its edge at one more victim gained thereby.

### 2

What else should he be set for, with his staff ?
    What, save to waylay with his lies, ensnare
    All travellers who might find him posted there,
And ask the road? I guessed what skull-like laugh     10
Would break, what crutch 'gin write my epitaph
    For pastime in the dusty thoroughfare,

### 3

If at his counsel I should turn aside
    Into that ominous tract which, all agree,
    Hides the Dark Tower. Yet acquiescingly     15
I did turn as he pointed: neither pride
Nor hope rekindling at the end descried,
    So much as gladness that some end might be.

### 4

For, what with my whole world-wide wandering,
    What with my search drawn out thro' years, my hope     20
    Dwindled into a ghost not fit to cope
With that obstreperous joy success would bring, –
I hardly tried now to rebuke the spring
    My heart made, finding failure in its scope.

### 5

As when a sick man very near to death     25
    Seems dead indeed, and feels begin and end
    The tears and takes the farewell of each friend,
And hears one bid the other go, draw breath
Freelier outside, ('since all is o'er,' he saith,
    'And the blow fallen no grieving can amend')     30

6

While some discuss if near the other graves
  Be room enough for this, and when a day
  Suits best for carrying the corpse away,
With care about the banners, scarves and staves, –
And still the man hears all, and only craves        35
  He may not shame such tender love and stay.

7

Thus, I had so long suffered in this quest,
  Heard failure prophesied so oft, been writ
  So many times among 'The Band' – to wit,
The knights who to the Dark Tower's search addressed    40
Their steps – that just to fail as they, seemed best,
  And all the doubt was now – should I be fit.

8

So, quiet as despair, I turned from him,
  That hateful cripple, out of his highway
  Into the path he pointed. All the day        45
Had been a dreary one at best, and dim
Was settling to its close, yet shot one grim
  Red leer to see the plain catch its estray.

9

For mark! no sooner was I fairly found
  Pledged to the plain, after a pace or two,        50
  Than pausing to throw backward a last view
O'er the safe road, 'twas gone! grey plain all round!
Nothing but plain to the horizon's bound.
  I might go on; naught else remained to do.

10

So on I went. I think I never saw        55
  Such starved ignoble nature; nothing throve:
  For flowers – as well expect a cedar grove!
But cockle, spurge, according to their law
Might propagate their kind, with none to awe,
  You'd think; a burr had been a treasure-trove.    60

11

No! penury, inertness and grimace,
  In some strange sort, were the land's portion. 'See
  Or shut your eyes' – said Nature peevishly –
'It nothing skills: I cannot help my case:
The Last Judgment's fire alone can cure this place,    65
  Calcine its clods and set my prisoners free.'

### 12

If there pushed any ragged thistle-stalk
    Above its mates, the head was chopped – the bents
    Were jealous else. What made those holes and rents
In the dock's harsh swarth leaves – bruised as to baulk    70
All hope of greenness? 'tis a brute must walk
    Pashing their life out, with a brute's intents.

### 13

As for the grass, it grew as scant as hair
    In leprosy – thin dry blades pricked the mud
    Which underneath looked kneaded up with blood.    75
One stiff blind horse, his every bone a-stare,
Stood stupefied, however he came there –
    Thrust out past service from the devil's stud!

### 14

Alive? he might be dead for aught I know,
    With that red gaunt and colloped neck a-strain,    80
    And shut eyes underneath the rusty mane.
Seldom went such grotesqueness with such woe:
I never saw a brute I hated so –
    He must be wicked to deserve such pain.

### 15

I shut my eyes and turned them on my heart.    85
    As a man calls for wine before he fights,
    I asked one draught of earlier, happier sights,
Ere fitly I could hope to play my part.
Think first, fight afterwards – the soldier's art:
    One taste of the old time sets all to rights.    90

### 16

Not it! I fancied Cuthbert's reddening face
    Beneath its garniture of curly gold,
    Dear fellow, till I almost felt him fold
An arm in mine to fix me to the place,
That way he used. Alas! one night's disgrace!    95
    Out went my heart's new fire and left it cold.

### 17

Giles, then, the soul of honour – there he stands
    Frank as ten years ago when knighted first.
    What honest man should dare (he said) he durst.
Good – but the scene shifts – faugh! what hangman's hands    100
Pin to his breast a parchment? his own bands
    Read it. Poor traitor, spit upon and curst!

### 18

Better this present than a past like that –
   Back therefore to my darkening path again.
   No sound, no sight as far as eye could strain.      105
Will the night send a howlet or a bat?
I asked: when something on the dismal flat
   Came to arrest my thoughts and change their train.

### 19

A sudden little river crossed my path
   As unexpected as a serpent comes.      110
   No sluggish tide congenial to the glooms –
This, as it frothed by, might have been a bath
For the fiend's glowing hoof – to see the wrath
   Of its black eddy bespate with flakes and spumes.

### 20

So petty yet so spiteful! All along,      115
   Low scrubby alders kneeled down over it;
   Drenched willows flung them headlong in a fit
Of mute despair, a suicidal throng:
The river which had done them all the wrong,
   Whate'er that was, rolled by, deterred no whit.      120

### 21

Which, while I forded, – good saints, how I feared
   To set my foot upon a dead man's cheek,
   Each step, or feel the spear I thrust to seek
For hollows, tangled in his hair or beard!
– It may have been a water-rat I speared,      125
   But, ugh! it sounded like a baby's shriek.

### 22

Glad was I when I reached the other bank.
   Now for a better country. Vain presage!
   Who were the strugglers, what war did they wage,
Whose savage trample thus could pad the dank      130
Soil to a plash? toads in a poisoned tank,
   Or wild cats in a red-hot iron cage –

### 23

The fight must so have seemed in that fell cirque.
   What penned them there, with all the plain to choose?
   No footprint leading to that horrid mews,      135
None out of it: mad brewage set to work
Their brains, no doubt, like galley-slaves the Turk
   Pits for his pastime, Christians against Jews.

### 24

And more than that – a furlong on – why, there!
   What bad use was that engine for, that wheel,         140
   Or brake, not wheel – that harrow fit to reel
Men's bodies out like silk? with all the air
Of Tophet's tool, on earth left unaware,
   Or brought to sharpen its rusty teeth of steel.

### 25

Then came a bit of stubbed ground, once a wood,        145
   Next a marsh, it would seem, and now mere earth
   Desperate and done with; (so a fool finds mirth,
Makes a thing and then mars it, till his mood
Changes and off he goes!) within a rood –
   Bog, clay and rubble, sand and stark black dearth.    150

### 26

Now blotches rankling, coloured gay and grim,
   Now patches where some leanness of the soil's
   Broke into moss or substances like boils;
Then came some palsied oak, a cleft in him
Like a distorted mouth that splits its rim         155
   Gaping at death, and dies while it recoils.

### 27

And just as far as ever from the end!
   Naught in the distance but the evening, nought
   To point my footstep further! At the thought,
A great black bird, Apollyon's bosom-friend,       160
Sailed past, nor beat his wide wing dragon-penned
   That brushed my cap – perchance the guide I sought.

### 28

For, looking up, aware I somehow grew,
   'Spite of the dusk, the plain had given place
   All round to mountains – with such name to grace    165
Mere ugly heights and heaps now stolen in view.
How thus they had surprised me, – solve it, you!
   How to get from them was no plain case.

### 29

Yet half I seemed to recognize some trick
   Of mischief happened to me, God knows when –    170
   In a bad dream perhaps. Here ended, then,
Progress this way. When, in the very nick
Of giving up, one time more, came a click
   As when a trap shuts – you're inside the den!

### 30

Burningly it came on me all at once,                    175
    This was the place! those two hills on the right,
    Crouched like two bulls locked horn in horn in fight –
While to the left, a tall scalped mountain . . . Dunce,
Fool, to be dozing at the very nonce,
    After a life spent training for the sight!             180

### 31

What in the midst lay but the Tower itself?
    The round squat turret, blind as the fool's heart,
    Built of brown stone, without a counterpart
In the whole world. The tempest's mocking elf
Points to the shipman thus the unseen shelf             185
    He strikes on, only when the timbers start.

### 32

Not see? because of night perhaps? – Why, day –
    Came back again for that! before it left,
    The dying sunset kindled through a cleft:
The hills, like giants at a hunting, lay –               190
    Chin upon hand, to see the game at bay, –
        'Now stab and end the creature – to the heft!'

### 33

Not hear? when noise was everywhere! it tolled
    Increasing like a bell. Names in my ears,
    Of all the lost adventures my peers, –                 195
How such a one was strong, and such was bold,
And such was fortunate, yet each of old
    Lost, lost! one moment knelled the woe of years.

### 34

There they stood, ranged along the hillsides – met
    To view the last of me, a living frame                 200
    For one more picture! in a sheet of flame
I saw them and I knew them all. And yet
Dauntless the slug-horn to my lips I set,
    And blew. '*Childe Roland to the Dark Tower came.*'

## Memorabilia

### 1

Ah, did you once see Shelley plain,
    And did he stop and speak to you?
And did you speak to him again?
    How strange it seems, and new!

### 2

But you were living before that,                                        5
   And also you are living after,
And the memory I started at –
   My starting moves your laughter!

### 3

I crossed a moor with a name of its own
   And a certain use in the world no doubt,    10
Yet a hand's-breadth of it shines alone
   'Mid the blank miles round about –

### 4

For there I picked up on the heather
   And there I put inside my breast
A moulted feather, an eagle-feather –                    15
   Well, I forget the rest.

## Andrea del Sarto

### *(Called 'The Faultless Painter')*

But do not let us quarrel any more,
No, my Lucrezia; bear with me for once:
Sit down and all shall happen as you wish.
You turn your face, but does it bring your heart?
I'll work then for your friend's friend, never fear,      5
Treat his own subject after his own way,
Fix his own time, accept too his own price,
And shut the money into this small hand
When next it takes mine. Will it? tenderly?
Oh, I'll content him, – but tomorrow, Love!               10
I often am much wearier than you think,
This evening more than usual, and it seems
As if – forgive now – should you let me sit
Here by the window with your hand in mine
And look a half-hour forth on Fiesole,                    15
Both of one mind, as married people use,
Quietly, quietly the evening through,
I might get up to-morrow to my work
Cheerful and fresh as ever. Let us try.
To-morrow, how you shall be glad for this!                20
Your soft hand is a woman of itself,
And mine the man's bared breast she curls inside.
Don't count the time lost, either; you must serve
For each of the five pictures we require –

It saves a model. So! keep looking so –                              25
My serpentining beauty, rounds on rounds!
– How could you ever prick those perfect ears,
Even to put the pearl there! oh, so sweet –
My face, my moon, my everybody's moon,
Which everybody looks on and calls his,                               30
And, I suppose, is looked on by in turn,
While she looks – no one's: very dear, no less!
You smile? why, there's my picture ready made,
There's what we painters call our harmony!
A common greyness silvers everything, –                              35
All in a twilight, you and I alike
– You, at the point of your first pride in me
(That's gone you know), – but I, at every point;
My youth, my hope, my art, being all toned down
To yonder sober pleasant Fiesole.                                    40
There's the bell clinking from the chapel-top;
That length of convent-wall across the way
Holds the trees safer, huddled more inside;
The last monk leaves the garden; days decrease,
And autumn grows, autumn in everything.                              45
Eh? the whole seems to fall into a shape
As if I saw alike my work and self
And all that I was born to be and do,
A twilight-piece. Love, we are in God's hand.
How strange now, looks the life he makes us lead!                    50
So free we seem, so fettered fast we are:
I feel he laid the fetter: let it lie!
This chamber for example – turn your head –
All that's behind us! you don't understand
Nor care to understand about my art,                                 55
But you can hear at least when people speak;
And that cartoon, the second from the door
– It is the thing, Love! so such things should be –
Behold Madonna, I am bold to say.
I can do with my pencil what I know,                                 60
What I see, what at bottom of my heart
I wish for, if I ever wish so deep –
Do easily, too – when I say perfectly
I do not boast, perhaps: yourself are judge,
Who listened to the Legate's talk last week,                         65
And just as much they used to say in France.
At any rate 'tis easy, all of it,
No sketches first, no studies, that's long past –
I do what many dream of all their lives
– Dream? strive to do, and agonise to do,                            70
And fail in doing. I could count twenty such
On twice your fingers, and not leave this town,

Who strive – you don't know how the others strive
To paint a little thing like that you smeared
Carelessly passing with your robes afloat,                    75
Yet do much less, so much less, some one says,
(I know his name, no matter) so much less!
Well, less is more, Lucrezia! I am judged.
There burns a truer light of God in them,
In their vexed, beating stuffed and stopped-up brain,          80
Heart, or whate'er else, than goes on to prompt
This low-pulsed forthright craftsman's hand of mine.
Their works drop groundward, but themselves, I know,
Reach many a time a heaven that's shut to me,
Enter and take their place there sure enough,                 85
Though they come back and cannot tell the world.
My works are nearer heaven, but I sit here.
The sudden blood of these men! at a word –
Praise them, it boils, or blame them, it boils too.
I, painting from myself and to myself,                        90
Know what I do, am unmoved by men's blame
Or their praise either. Somebody remarks
Morello's outline there is wrongly traced,
His hue mistaken; what of that? or else,
Rightly traced and well ordered; what of that?                95
Ah, but a man's reach should exceed his grasp,
Or what's a Heaven for? All is silver-grey
Placid and perfect with my art – the worse!
I know both what I want and what might gain –
And yet how profitless to know, to sigh                       100
'Had I been two, another and myself,
Our head would have o'erlooked the world!' No doubt.
Yonder's a work now, of that famous youth
The Urbinate who died five years ago.
('Tis copied, George Vasari sent it me.)                      105
Well, I can fancy how he did it all,
Pouring his soul, with kings and popes to see,
Reaching, that Heaven might so replenish him,
Above and through his art – for it gives way;
That arm is wrongly put – and there again –                   110
A fault to pardon in the drawing's lines,
Its body, so to speak! its soul is right,
He means right – that, a child may understand.
Still, what an arm! and I could alter it.
But all the play, the insight and the stretch –              115
Out of me! out of me! And wherefore out?
Had you enjoined them on me, given me soul,
We might have risen to Rafael, I and you.
Nay, Love, you did give all I asked, I think –
More than I merit, yes, by many times.                        120

But had you – oh, with the same perfect brow,
And perfect eyes, and more than perfect mouth,
And the low voice my soul hears, as a bird
The fowler's pipe, and follows to the snare –
Had you, with these the same, but brought a mind!                    125
Some women do so. Had the mouth there urged
'God and the glory! never care for gain.
The present by the future, what is that?
Live for fame, side by side with Angelo –
Rafael is waiting: up to God, all three!'                            130
I might have done it for you. So it seems –
Perhaps not. All is as God over-rules.
Beside, incentives come from the soul's self;
The rest avail not. Why do I need you?
What wife had Rafael, or has Angelo?                                  135
In this world, who can do a thing, will not –
And who would do it, cannot, I perceive:
Yet the will's somewhat – somewhat, too, the power –
And thus we half-men struggle. At the end,
God, I conclude, compensates, punishes.                              140
'Tis safer for me, if the award be strict,
That I am something underrated here,
Poor this long while, despised, to speak the truth.
I dared not, do you know, leave home all day,
For fear of chancing on the Paris lords.                             145
The best is when they pass and look aside;
But they speak sometimes; I must bear it all.
Well may they speak! That Francis, that first time,
And that long festal year at Fontainebleau!
I surely then could sometimes leave the ground,                      150
Put on the glory, Rafael's daily wear,
In that humane great monarch's golden look, –
One finger in his beard or twisted curl
Over his mouth's good mark that made the smile,
One arm about my shoulder, round my neck,                            155
The jingle of his gold chain in my ear,
You painting proudly with his breath on me,
All his court round him, seeing with his eyes,
Such frank French eyes, and such a fire of souls
Profuse, my hand kept plying by those hearts, –                      160
And, best of all, this, this, this face beyond,
This in the background, waiting on my work,
To crown the issue with a last reward!
A good time, was it not, my kingly days?
And had you not grown restless – but I know –                        165
'Tis done and past; 'twas right, my instinct said;
Too live the life grew, golden and not grey –
And I'm the weak-eyed bat no sun should tempt

Out of the grange whose four walls make his world.
How could it end in any other way?                                    170
You called me, and I came home to your heart.
The triumph was to have ended there – then if
I reached it ere the triumph, what is lost?
Let my hands frame your face in your hair's gold,
You beautiful Lucrezia that are mine!                                 175
'Rafael did this, Andrea painted that;
The Roman's is the better when you pray,
But still the other's Virgin was his wife –'
Men will excuse me. I am glad to judge
Both pictures in your presence; clearer grows                        180
My better fortune, I resolve to think.
For, do you know, Lucrezia, as God lives,
Said one day Angelo, his very self,
To Rafael . . . I have known it all these years . . .
(When the young man was flaming out his thoughts                     185
Upon a palace-wall for Rome to see,
Too lifted up in heart because of it)
'Friend, there's a certain sorry little scrub
Goes up and down our Florence, none cares how,
Who, were he set to plan and execute                                 190
As you are pricked on by your popes and kings,
Would bring the sweat into that brow of yours!'
To Rafael's! – And indeed the arm is wrong.
I hardly dare – yet, only you to see,
Give the chalk here – quick, thus the line should go!                195
Ay, but the soul! he's Rafael! rub it out!
Still, all I care for, if he spoke the truth,
(What he? why, who but Michel Angelo?
Do you forget already words like those?)
If really there was such a chance, so lost,                          200
Is, whether you're – not grateful – but more pleased.
Well, let me think so. And you smile indeed!
This hour has been an hour! Another smile?
If you would sit thus by me every night
I should work better, do you comprehend?                             205
I mean that I should earn more, give you more.
See, it is settled dusk now; there's a star;
Morello's gone, the watch-lights show the wall,
The cue-owls speak the name we call them by.
Come from the window, Love, – come in, at last,                      210
Inside the melancholy little house
We built to be so gay with. God is just.
King Francis may forgive me. Oft at nights
When I look up from painting, eyes tired out,
The walls become illumined, brick from brick                         215
Distinct, instead of mortar fierce bright gold,

That gold of his I did cement them with!
Let us but love each other. Must you go?
That Cousin here again? he waits outside?
Must see you – you, and not with me? Those loans!          220
More gaming debts to pay? you smiled for that?
Well, let smiles buy me! have you more to spend?
While hand and eye and something of a heart
Are left me, work's my ware, and what's it worth?
I'll pay my fancy. Only let me sit                         225
The grey remainder of the evening out,
Idle, you call it, and muse perfectly
How I could paint, were I but back in France,
One picture, just one more – the Virgin's face,
Not yours this time! I want you at my side                 230
To hear them – that is, Michel Angelo –
Judge all I do and tell you of its worth.
Will you? Tomorrow, satisfy your friend.
I take the subjects for his corridor,
Finish the portrait out of hand – there, there,           235
And throw him in another thing or two
If he demurs; the whole should prove enough
To pay for this same Cousin's freak. Beside,
What's better and what's all I care about,
Get you the thirteen scudi for the ruff!                   240
Love, does that please you? Ah, but what does he,
The Cousin! what does he to please you more?

I am grown peaceful as old age tonight.
I regret little, I would change still less.
Since there my past life lies, why alter it?              245
The very wrong to Francis! it is true
I took his coin, was tempted and complied,
And built this house and sinned, and all is said.
My father and my mother died of want.
Well, had I riches of my own? you see                     250
How one gets rich! Let each one bear his lot.
They were born poor, lived poor, and poor they died:
And I have laboured somewhat in my time
And not been paid profusely. Some good son
Paint my two hundred pictures – let him try!              255
No doubt, there's something strikes a balance. Yes,
You loved me quite enough, it seems to-night.
This must suffice me here. What would one have?
In heaven, perhaps, new chances, one more chance –
Four great walls in the New Jerusalem,                    260
Meted on each side by the angel's reed,
For Leonard, Rafael, Angelo and me
To cover – the three first without a wife,

While I have mine! So – still they overcome
Because there's still Lucrezia, – as I choose.                    265

Again the Cousin's whistle! Go, my Love.

# Two in the Campagna

### 1

I wonder do you feel today
   As I have felt, since, hand in hand,
We sat down on the grass, to stray
   In spirit better through the land,
This morn of Rome and May?                                      5

### 2

For me, I touched a thought, I know,
   Has tantalised me many times,
(Like turns of thread the spiders throw
   Mocking across our path) for rhymes
To catch at and let go.                                         10

### 3

Help me to hold it: first it left
   The yellowing fennel, run to seed
There, branching from the brickwork's cleft,
   Some old tomb's ruin: yonder weed
Took up the floating weft,                                      15

### 4

Where one small orange cup amassed
   Five beetles, – blind and green they grope
Among the honey-meal, – and last
   Everywhere on the grassy slope
I traced it. Hold it fast!                                      20

### 5

The champaign with its endless fleece
   Of feathery grasses everywhere!
Silence and passion, joy and peace,
   An everlasting wash of air –
Rome's ghost since her decease.                                 25

### 6

Such life there, through such lengths of hours,
   Such miracles performed in play,
Such primal naked forms of flowers,
   Such letting Nature have her way
While Heaven looks from its towers.                             30

### 7

How say you? Let us, O my dove,
  Let us be unashamed of soul,
As earth lies bare to heaven above.
  How is it under our control
To love or not to love?                                          35

### 8

I would that you were all to me,
  You that are just so much, no more –
Nor yours, nor mine, – nor slave nor free!
  Where does the fault lie? what the core
Of the wound, since wound must be?                              40

### 9

I would I could adopt your will,
  See with your eyes, and set my heart
Beating by yours, and drink my fill
  At your soul's springs, – your part my part
In life, for good and ill.                                      45

### 10

No. I yearn upward – touch you close,
  Then stand away. I kiss your cheek,
Catch your soul's warmth, – I pluck the rose
  And love it more than tongue can speak –
Then the good minute goes.                                      50

### 11

Already how am I so far
  Out of that minute? Must I go
Still like the thistle-ball, no bar,
  Onward, whenever light winds blow,
Fixed by no friendly star?                                      55

### 12

Just when I seemed about to learn!
  Where is the thread now? Off again!
The old trick! Only I discern –
  Infinite passion, and the pain
Of finite hearts that yearn.                                    60

# A Grammarian's Funeral

*Time – Shortly after the Revival of Learning in Europe*

Let us begin and carry up this corpse,
  Singing together.

Leave we the common crofts, the vulgar thorpes
    Each in its tether
Sleeping safe on the bosom of the plain,                    5
    Cared-for till cock-crow:
Look out if yonder be not day again
    Rimming the rock-row!
That's the appropriate country – there, man's thought,
    Rarer, intenser,                                        10
Self-gathered for an outbreak, as it ought,
    Chafes in the censer.
Leave we the unlettered plain its herd and crop;
    Seek we sepulture
On a tall mountain, cited to the top,                       15
    Crowded with culture!
All the peaks soar, but one the rest excels;
    Clouds overcome it;
No, yonder sparkle is the citadel's
    Circling its summit!                                    20
Thither our path lies – wind we up the heights –
    Wait ye the warning?
Our low life was the level's and the night's;
    He's for the morning!
Step to a tune, square chests, erect each head,            25
    'Ware the beholders!
This is our master, famous calm and dead,
    Borne on our shoulders.

Sleep, crop and herd! sleep, darkling thorpe and croft,
    Safe from the weather!                                  30
He, whom we convoy to his grave aloft,
    Singing together,
He was a man born with thy face and throat,
    Lyric Apollo!
Long he lived nameless: how should spring take note         35
    Winter would follow?
Till lo, the little touch, and youth was gone!
    Cramped and diminished,
Moaned he, 'New measures, other feet anon!
    My dance is finished?'                                  40
No, that's the world's way! (keep the mountainside,
    Make for the city.)
He knew the signal, and stepped on with pride
    Over men's pity;
Left play for work, and grappled with the world            45
    Bent on escaping:
'What's in the scroll,' quoth he, 'thou keepest furled?
    Show me their shaping,
Theirs, who most studied man, the bard and sage, –

Give!' – So, he gowned him,                                           50
    Straight got by heart that book to its last page:
      Learned, we found him!
Yea, but we found him bald too – eyes like lead,
      Accents uncertain:
'Time to taste life,' another would have said,                       55
      'Up with the curtain!'
This man said rather, 'Actual life comes next?
      Patience a moment!
Grant I have mastered learning's crabbed text,
      Still there's the comment.                                60
Let me know all. Prate not of most or least,
      Painful or easy:
Even to the crumbs I'd fain eat up the feast,
      Ay, nor feel queasy!'
Oh, such a life as he resolved to live,                              65
      When he had learned it,
When he had gathered all books had to give;
      Sooner, he spurned it!
Image the whole, then execute the parts –
      Fancy the fabric                                         70
Quite, ere you build, ere steel strike fire from quartz,
      Ere mortar dab brick!

(Here's the town-gate reached: there's the market-place
      Gaping before us.)
Yea, this in him was the peculiar grace                              75
      (Hearten our chorus)
Still before living he'd learn how to live –
      No end to learning.
Earn the means first – God surely will contrive
      Use for our earning.                                     80
Others mistrust and say – 'But time escapes, –
      Live now or never!'
He said, 'What's Time? leave Now for dogs and apes!
      Man has For ever.'
Back to his book then: deeper drooped his head:                     85
      *Calculus* racked him:
Leaden before, his eyes grew dross of lead:
      *Tussis* attacked him.
'Now, Master, take a little rest!' – not he!
      (Caution redoubled!                                      90
Step two a-breast, the way winds narrowly.)
      Not a whit troubled
Back to his studies, fresher than at first,
      Fierce as a dragon
He (soul-hydroptic with a sacred thirst)                            95
      Sucked at the flagon.

Oh, if we draw a circle premature,
   Heedless of far gain,
Greedy for quick returns of profit, sure
   Bad is our bargain!                       100
Was it not great? did not he throw on God,
   (He loves the burthen) –
God's task to make the heavenly period
   Perfect the earthen?
Did not he magnify the mind, shew clear         105
   Just what it all meant?
He would not discount life, as fools do here,
   Paid by instalment!
He ventured neck or nothing – heaven's success
   Found, or earth's failure:             110
'Wilt thou trust death or not?' he answered 'Yes.
   'Hence with life's pale lure!'
That low man seeks a little thing to do,
   Sees it and does it:
This high man, with a great thing to pursue,    115
   Dies ere he knows it.
That low man goes on adding one to one,
   His hundred's soon hit:
This high man, aiming at a million,
   Misses an unit.                  120
That, has the world here – should he need the next,
   Let the world mind him!
This, throws himself on God, and unperplext
   Seeking shall find Him.
So, with the throttling hands of Death at strife,    125
   Ground he at grammar;
Still, through the rattle, parts of speech were rife.
   While he could stammer
He settled *Hoti's* business – let it be! –
   Properly based *Oun* –            130
Gave us the doctrine of the enclitic *De*,
   Dead from the waist down.
Well, here's the platform, here's the proper place:
   Hail to your purlieus
All ye highfliers of the feathered race,       135
   Swallows and curlews!
Here's the top-peak! the multitude below
   Live, for they can, there.
This man decided not to Live but Know –
   Bury this man there?            140
Here – here's his place, where meteors shoot, clouds form,
   Lightnings are loosened,
Stars come and go! let joy break with the storm –
   Peace let the dew send!

Lofty designs must close in like effects:                    145
    Loftily lying,
Leave him – still loftier than the world suspects,
    Living and dying.


## Never the Time and the Place

    Never the time and the place
    And the loved one all together!
    This path – how soft to pace!
    This May – what magic weather!
      Where is the loved one's face?                    5
  In a dream that loved one's face meets mine,
  But the house is narrow, the place is bleak
Where, outside, rain and wind combine
  With a furtive ear, if I strive to speak,
  With a hostile eye at my flushing cheek,                    10
With a malice that marks each word, each sign!
O enemy sly and serpentine,
    Uncoil thee from the waking man!
      Do I hold the Past
        Thus firm and fast                    15
    Yet doubt if the Future hold I can?
    This path so soft to pace shall lead
    Thro' the magic of May to herself indeed!
    Or narrow if needs the house must be,
    Outside are the storms and strangers: we –                    20
    Oh, close, safe, warm sleep I and she,
    – I and she!

# Emily (Jane) Brontë
# (1818–1848)

## 'What winter floods, what showers of spring'

What winter floods, what showers of spring
Have drenched the grass by night and day
And yet beneath that spectre ring
Unmoved and undiscovered lay

A mute remembrancer of crime                                    5
Long lost concealed forgot for years
It comes at last to cancel time
And waken unavailing tears

## 'Long neglect has worn away'

Long neglect has worn away
Half the sweet enchanting smile
Time has turned the bloom to grey
Mould and damp the face defile

But that lock of silky hair                                     5
Still beneath the picture twined
Tells what once those features were
Paints their image on the mind

Fair the hand that traced that line
'Dearest ever deem me true'                                    10
Swiftly flew the fingers fine
When the pen that motto drew

## 'The night is darkening round me'

The night is darkening round me
The wild winds coldly blow
But a tyrant spell has bound me
And I cannot, cannot go

The giant trees are bending                              5
Their bare boughs weighed with snow
And the storm is fast descending
And yet I cannot go

Clouds beyond cloud above me,
Wastes beyond wastes below,                              10
But nothing drear can move me,
I will not, cannot go

## 'All hushed and still within the house'

All hushed and still within the house
Without – all wind and driving rain
But something whispers to my mind
Through rain and [through the] wailing wind
          – Never again                                  5
Never again? Why not again?
Memory has power as real as thine

## 'O Dream, where art thou now?'

O Dream, where art thou now?
Long years have passed away
Since last from off thine angel brow
I saw the light decay –

Alas, alas for me                                        5
Thou wert so bright and fair
I could not think thy memory
Would yield me nought but care!

The sun-beam and the storm,
The summer-eve divine,                                   10
The silent night of solemn calm,
The full moon's cloudless shine

Were once entwined with thee
But now, with weary pain –
Lost vision! 'tis enough for me –                        15
Thou canst not shine again.

## 'How still, how happy! those are words'

How still, how happy! those are words
That once would scarce agree together

I loved the plashing of the surge –
The changing heaven, the breezy weather,

More than smooth seas and cloudless skies                           5
And solemn, soothing, softened airs
That in the forest woke no sighs
And from the green spray shook no tears

How still, how happy! now I feel
Where silence dwells is sweeter far                                 10
Than laughing mirth's most joyous swell
However pure its raptures are

Come sit down on this sunny stone
'Tis wintery light o'er flowerless moors –
But sit – for we are all alone                                      15
And clear expand heaven's breathless shores

I could think in the withered grass
Spring's budding wreaths we might discern
The violet's eye might shyly flash
And young leaves shoot among the fern                               20

It is but thought – full many a night
The snow shall clothe those hills afar
And storms shall add a drearier blight
And winds shall wage a wilder war

Before the lark may herald in                                       25
Fresh foliage twined with blossoms fair
And summer days again begin
Their glory-haloed crown to wear

Yet my heart loves December's smile
As much as July's golden beam                                       30
Then let us sit and watch the while
The blue ice curdling on the stream –

## 'Mild the mist upon the hill'

Mild the mist upon the hill
Telling not of storms tomorrow
No, the day has wept its fill
Spent its store of silent sorrow

Oh I'm gone back to the days of youth                               5
I am a child once more

And 'neath my father's sheltering roof
And near the old hall door

I watch this cloudy evening fall
After a day of rain                                               10
Blue mists, sweet mists of summer pall
The horizon's mountain chain

The damp stands on the long green grass
As thick as morning's tears
And dreamy scents of fragrance pass                              15
That breathe of other years

## 'Come, walk with me'

Come, walk with me,
There's only thee
To bless my spirit now –
We used to love on winter nights
To wander through the snow;                                       5
Can we not woo back old delights?
The clouds rush dark and wild
They fleck with shade our mountain heights
The same as long ago
And on the horizon rest at last                                  10
In looming masses piled;
While moonbeams flash and fly so fast
We scarce can say they smiled –

Come walk with me, come walk with me;
We were not once so few                                           15
But Death has stolen our company
As sunshine steals the dew –
He took them one by one and we
Are left the only two;
So closer would my feelings twine                                20
Because they have no stay but thine –

'Nay call me not – it may not be
Is human love so true?
Can Friendship's flower droop on for years
And then revive anew?                                            25
No, though the soil be wet with tears,
How fair soe'er it grew
The vital sap once perished
Will never flow again
And surer than that dwelling dread,                             30

The narrow dungeon of the dead
Time parts the hearts of men –'

# To Imagination

When weary with the long day's care,
And earthly change from pain to pain,
And lost and ready to despair,
Thy kind voice calls me back again:
Oh, my true friend! I am not lone,                           5
While thou canst speak with such a tone!

So hopeless is the world without;
The world within I doubly prize;
Thy world, where guile, and hate, and doubt,
And cold suspicion never rise;                               10
Where thou, and I, and Liberty,
Have undisputed sovereignty.

What matters it, that, all around,
Danger, and guilt, and darkness lie,
If but within our bosom's bound                              15
We hold a bright, untroubled sky,
Warm with ten thousand mingled rays
Of suns that know no winter days?

Reason, indeed, may oft complain
For Nature's sad reality                                     20
And tell the suffering heart how vain
Its cherished dreams must always be;
And Truth may rudely trample down
The flowers of Fancy, newly-blown:

But, thou art ever there, to bring                          25
The hovering vision back, and breathe
New glories o'er the blighted spring
And call a lovelier Life from Death,
And whisper, with a voice divine,
Of real worlds, as bright as thine.                         30

I trust not to thy phantom bliss,
Yet, still, in evening's quiet hour,
With never-failing thankfulness,
I welcome thee, Benignant Power;
Sure solacer of human cares,                                35
And sweeter hope, when hope despairs!

# Remembrance

### (also known as 'R. Alcona to J. Brenzaida')

Cold in the earth and the deep snow piled above thee!
Far, far removed, cold in the dreary grave:
Have I forgot, my only Love, to love thee,
Severed at last by Time's all-severing wave?

Now, when alone, do my thoughts no longer hover          5
Over the mountains on Angora's shore;
Resting their wings where heath and fern-leaves cover
That noble heart for ever, ever more?

Cold in the earth, and fifteen wild Decembers
From those brown hills have melted into spring –         10
Faithful indeed is the spirit that remembers
After such years of change and suffering!

Sweet Love of youth, forgive if I forget thee
While the World's tide is bearing me along:
Other desires and other Hopes beset me,                  15
Hopes which obscure but cannot do thee wrong.

No later light has lightened up my heaven;
No second morn has ever shone for me;
All my life's bliss from thy dear life was given –
All my life's bliss is in the grave with thee.           20

But when the days of golden dreams had perished
And even Despair was powerless to destroy,
Then did I learn how existence could be cherished,
Strengthened and fed without the aid of joy.

Then did I check the tears of useless passion,           25
Weaned my young soul from yearning after thine;
Sternly denied its burning wish to hasten
Down to that tomb already more than mine!

And even yet, I dare not let it languish,
Dare not indulge in Memory's rapturous pain;            30
Once drinking deep of that divinest anguish,
How could I seek the empty world again?

# Julian M. and A. G. Rochelle

## (also known as 'The Prisoner')

Silent is the House – all are laid asleep;
One, alone, looks out o'er the snow-wreaths deep;
Watching every cloud, dreading every breeze
That whirls the 'wildering drifts and bends the groaning trees.

Cheerful is the hearth, soft the matted floor;                     5
Not one shivering gust creeps through pane or door;
The little lamp burns straight, its rays shoot strong and far:
I trim it well to be the Wanderer's guiding-star.

Frown, my haughty Sire; chide, my angry Dame;
Set your slaves to spy, threaten me with shame;                    10
But neither sire nor dame, nor prying serf shall know
What angel nightly tracks that waste of winter snow.

In the dungeon-crypts idly did I stray
Reckless of the lives wasting there away;
'Draw the ponderous bars, open Warder stern!'                      15
He dare not say me nay – the hinges harshly turn.

'Our guests are darkly lodged,' I whispered gazing through
The vault whose grated eye showed heaven more grey than blue
(This was when glad Spring laughed in awaking pride);
'Aye, darkly lodged enough!' returned my sullen guide.             20

Then, God forgive my youth, forgive my careless tongue!
I scoffed as the chill chains on the damp flagstones rung;
'Confined in triple walls, art thou so much to fear,
That we must bind thee down and clench thy fetters here?'

The captive raised her face, it was as soft and mild               25
As sculptured marble saint or slumbering, unweaned child;
It was so soft and mild, it was so sweet and fair
Pain could not trace a line nor grief a shadow there!

The captive raised her hand and pressed it to her brow:
'I have been struck,' she said, 'and I am suffering now;           30
Yet these are little worth, your bolts and irons strong;
And were they forged in steel they could not hold me long.'

Hoarse laughed the jailor grim, 'Shall I be won to hear;
Dost think fond, dreaming wretch that *I* shall grant thy prayer?
Or better still, wilt melt my master's heart with groans?                    35
Ah sooner might the sun thaw down these granite stones!

My master's voice is low, his aspect bland and kind,
But hard as hardest flint the soul that lurks behind:
And I am rough and rude, yet, not more rough to see
Than is the hidden ghost which has its home in me!'                          40

About her lips there played a smile of almost scorn:
'My friend,' she gently said, 'you have not heard me mourn;
When you my parents' lives – *my* lost life can restore,
Then may I weep and sue – but, never, Friend, before!'

Her head sank on her hands, its fair curls swept the ground;        45
The dungeon seemed to swim in strange confusion round.
'Is she so near to death?' I murmured, half aloud,
And kneeling, parted back the floating golden cloud.

Alas, how former days upon my heart were borne,
How memory mirrored then the prisoner's joyous morn –                  50
Too blithe, too loving Child, too warmly, wildly gay!
Was that the wintry close of thy celestial May?

She knew me and she sighed, 'Lord Julian, can it be,
Of all my playmates, you, alone, remember me?
Nay start not at my words, unless you deem it shame                     55
To own from conquered foe, a once familiar name –

I can not wonder now at ought the world will do,
And insult and contempt I lightly brook from you,
Since those who vowed away their souls to win my love
Around this living grave like utter strangers move:                        60

Nor has one voice been raised to plead that I might die
Not buried under earth but in the open sky;
By ball or speedy knife or headsman's skilful blow –
A quick and welcome pang instead of lingering woe!

Yet, tell them, Julian, all, I am not doomed to wear                     65
Year after year in gloom and desolate despair;
A messenger of Hope comes every night to me,
And offers, for short life, eternal liberty.

He comes with western winds, with evening's wandering airs,
With that clear dusk of heaven that brings the thickest stars;         70
Winds take a pensive tone and stars a tender fire,
And visions rise and change which kill me with desire –

Desire for nothing known in my maturer years
When joy grew mad with awe at counting future tears;
When, if my spirit's sky was full of flashes warm,                    75
I knew not whence they came, from sun or thunderstorm;

But first a hush of peace, a soundless calm descends;
The struggle of distress and fierce impatience ends;
Mute music soothes my breast – unuttered harmony
That I could never dream till earth was lost to me.                    80

Then dawns the Invisible, the Unseen its truth reveals;
My outward sense is gone, my inward essence feels –
Its wings are almost free, its home, its harbour found;
Measuring the gulf it stoops and dares the final bound!

O, dreadful is the check – intense the agony                          85
When the ear begins to hear and the eye begins to see,
When the pulse begins to throb, the brain to think again,
The soul to feel the flesh and the flesh to feel the chain!

Yet I would lose no sting, would wish no torture less;
The more that anguish racks the earlier it will bless:                90
And robed in fires of Hell, or bright with heavenly shine
If it but herald Death, the vision is divine.'

She ceased to speak and I, unanswering, watched her there,
Not daring now to touch one lock of silken hair –
As I had knelt in scorn, on the dank floor I knelt still,             95
My fingers in the links of that iron hard and chill.

I heard and yet heard not the surly keeper growl;
I saw, yet did not see, the flagstones damp and foul;
The keeper, to and fro, paced by the bolted door
And shivered as he walked and as he shivered, swore –                 100

While my cheek glowed in flame, I marked that he did rave
Of air that froze his blood and moisture like the grave –
'We have been two hours good!' he muttered peevishly,
Then, loosing off his belt the rusty dungeon key,

He said, 'You may be pleased, Lord Julian, still to stay,             105
But duty will not let me linger here all day;
If I might go, I'd leave this badge of mine with you
Not doubting that you'd prove a jailor stern and true.'

I took the proffered charge; the captive's drooping lid
Beneath its shady lash a sudden lightning hid.                        110
Earth's hope was not so dead, heaven's home was not so dear:
I read it in that flash of longing quelled by fear.

Then like a tender child whose hand did just enfold
Safe in its eager grasp a bird it wept to hold,
When pierced with one wild glance from the troubled hazel eye          115
It gushes into tears and lets its treasure fly,

Thus ruth and selfish love together striving tore
The heart all newly taught to pity and adore;
If I should break the chain I felt my bird would go;
Yet I must break the chain or seal the prisoner's woe.                 120

Short strife! what rest could soothe – what peace could visit me
While she lay pining there for Death to set her free?
'Rochelle, the dungeons teem with foes to gorge our hate –
Thou art too young to die by such a bitter fate!'

With hurried blow on blow I struck the fetters through                 125
Regardless how that deed my after hours might rue.
Oh, I was over-blest by the warm unasked embrace –
By the smile of grateful joy that lit her angel face!

And I was over-blest – aye, more than I could dream –
When, faint, she turned aside from noon's unwonted beam;               130
When though the cage was wide – the heaven around it lay –
Its pinion would not waft my wounded dove away.

Through thirteen anxious weeks of terror-blent delight
I guarded her by day and guarded her by night,
While foes were prowling near and Death gazed greedily                 135
And only Hope remained a faithful friend to me.

Then oft with taunting smile, I heard my kindred tell
'How Julian loved his hearth and sheltering rooftree well;
How the trumpet's voice might call, the battle-standard wave
But Julian had no heart to fill a patriot's grave.'                    140

And I, who am so quick to answer sneer with sneer;
So ready to condemn, to scorn a coward's fear –
I held my peace like one whose conscience keeps him dumb
And saw my kinsmen go – and lingered still at home.

Another hand than mine my rightful banner held                         145
And gathered my renown on Freedom's crimson field;
Yet I had no desire the glorious prize to gain –
It needed braver nerve to face the world's disdain.

And by the patient strength that could that world defy;
By suffering, with calm mind, contempt and calumny;                   150
By never-doubting love, unswerving constancy,
Rochelle, I earned at last an equal love from thee!

## 'No coward soul is mine'

No coward soul is mine
No trembler in the world's storm-troubled sphere
I see Heaven's glories shine
And Faith shines equal arming me from Fear

O God within my breast                                           5
Almighty ever-present Deity
Life, that in me hast rest
As I Undying Life, have power in thee

Vain are the thousand creeds
That move men's hearts, unutterably vain,                        10
Worthless as withered weeds
Or idlest froth amid the boundless main

To waken doubt in one
Holding so fast by thy infinity
So surely anchored on                                            15
The steadfast rock of Immortality

With wide-embracing love
Thy Spirit animates eternal years
Pervades and broods above,
Changes, sustains, dissolves, creates and rears                  20

Though Earth and moon were gone
And suns and universes ceased to be
And thou wert left alone
Every Existence would exist in thee

There is not room for Death                                      25
Nor atom that his might could render void
Since thou are Being and Breath
And what thou art may never be destroyed

# *Arthur Hugh Clough (1819–1861)*

## 'Say not the struggle naught availeth'

Say not the struggle naught availeth,
   The labor and the wounds are vain,
The enemy faints not nor faileth,
   And as things have been, things remain.

If hopes were dupes, fears may be liars;           5
   It may be, in yon smoke concealed,
Your comrades chase e'en now the fliers,
   And, but for you, possess the field.

For while the tired waves vainly breaking,
   Seem here no painful inch to gain,           10
Far back through creeks and inlets making
   Comes silent, flooding in, the main,

And not by eastern windows only,
   When daylight comes, comes in the light,
In front the sun climbs slow, how slowly,          15
   But westward, look! the land is bright.

## 'That there are powers above us I admit'

That there are powers above us I admit;
It may be true too
That while we walk the troublous tossing sea,
That when we see the o'ertopping waves advance,
And when [we] feel our feet beneath us sink,          5
There are who walk beside us; and the cry
That rises so spontaneous to the lips,
The 'Help us or we perish,' is not nought,
An evanescent spectrum of disease.
It may be that in deed and not in fancy,          10
A hand that is not ours upstays our steps,
A voice that is not ours commands the waves,
Commands the waves, and whispers in our ear,

O thou of little faith, why didst thou doubt?
At any rate –                                          15
That there are beings above us, I believe,
And when we lift up holy hands of prayer,
I will not say they will not give us aid.

# Matthew Arnold
## (1822–1888)

### To Marguerite

#### In Returning a Volume of the Letters of Ortis

Yes: in the sea of life enisled,
With echoing straits between us thrown,
Dotting the shoreless watery wild,
We mortal millions live *alone*.
The islands feel the enclasping flow,      5
And then their endless bounds they know.

But when the moon their hollows lights,
And they are swept by balms of spring,
And in their glens, on starry nights,
The nightingales divinely sing,      10
And lovely notes, from shore to shore,
Across the sounds and channels pour;

Oh then a longing like despair
Is to their farthest caverns sent;
– For surely once, they feel, we were      15
Parts of a single continent.
Now round us spreads the watery plain –
Oh might our marges meet again!

Who ordered, that their longing's fire
Should be, as soon as kindled, cooled?      20
Who renders vain their deep desire?
A God, a God their severance ruled!
And bade betwixt their shores to be
The unplumbed, salt, estranging sea.

### Self-Dependence

Weary of myself, and sick of asking
What I am, and what I ought to be,
At this vessel's prow I stand, which bears me
Forwards, forwards, o'er the starlit sea.

And a look of passionate desire                                    5
O'er the sea and to the stars I send:
'Ye who from my childhood up have calmed me,
Calm me, ah, compose me to the end.

'Ah, once more,' I cried, 'ye Stars, ye Waters,
On my heart your mighty charm renew:                               10
Still, still let me, as I gaze upon you,
Feel my soul becoming vast like you.'

From the intense, clear, star-sown vault of heaven,
Over the lit sea's unquiet way,
In the rustling night-air came the answer –                        15
'Wouldst thou *be* as these are? *Live* as they.

'Unaffrighted by the silence round them,
Undistracted by the sights they see,
These demand not that the things without them
Yield them love, amusement, sympathy.                              20

'And with joy the stars perform their shining,
And the sea its long moon-silvered roll;
For alone they live, nor pine with noting
All the fever of some differing soul.

'Bounded by themselves, and unobservant                            25
In what state God's other works may be,
In their own tasks all their powers pouring,
These attain the mighty life you see.'

O air-born Voice! long since, severely clear,
A cry like thine in mine own heart I hear.                         30
'Resolve to be thyself; and know that he,
Who finds himself, loses his misery!'

# Dover Beach

The sea is calm tonight.
The tide is full, the moon lies fair
Upon the Straits; on the French coast, the light
Gleams, and is gone; the cliffs of England stand,
Glimmering and vast, out in the tranquil bay.                      5
Come to the window, sweet is the night air!
Only, from the long line of spray
Where the ebb meets the moon-blanched land,
Listen! you hear the grating roar
Of pebbles which the waves suck back, and fling,                   10

At their return, up the high strand,
Begin, and cease, and then again begin,
With tremulous cadence slow, and bring
The eternal note of sadness in.

Sophocles long ago                                    15
Heard it on the Ægean, and it brought
Into his mind the turbid ebb and flow
Of human misery; we
Find also in the sound a thought,
Hearing it by this distant northern sea.              20

The sea of faith
Was once, too, at the full, and round earth's shore
Lay like the folds of a bright girdle furled;
But now I only hear
Its melancholy, long withdrawing roar,                25
Retreating to the breath
Of the night-wind, down the vast edges drear
And naked shingles of the world.

Ah, love, let us be true
To one another! for the world, which seems            30
To lie before us like a land of dreams,
So various, so beautiful, so new,
Hath really neither joy, nor love, nor light,
Nor certitude, nor peace, nor help for pain;
And we are here as on a darkling plain                35
Swept with confused alarms of struggle and flight,
Where ignorant armies clash by night.

# The Scholar-Gipsy

'There was very lately a lad in the University of Oxford, who was by his poverty forced to leave his studies there; and at last to join himself to a company of vagabond gipsies. Among these extravagant people, by the insinuating subtilty of his carriage, he quickly got so much of their love and esteem as that they discovered to him their mystery. After he had been a pretty while well exercised in the trade, there chanced to ride by a couple of scholars, who had formerly been of his acquaintance. They quickly spied out their old friend among the gipsies; and he gave them an account of the necessity which drove him to that kind of life, and told them that the people he went with were not such impostors as they were taken for, but that they had a traditional kind of learning among them, and could do wonders by the power of imagination, their fancy binding that of others: that himself had learned much of their art, and when he had compassed the whole secret, he intended, he said, to leave their company, and give the world an account of what he had learned.' – *Glanvil's Vanity of Dogmatizing*, 1661.

Go, for they call you, Shepherd, from the hill;
  Go, Shepherd, and untie the wattled cotes:
    No longer leave thy wistful flock unfed,
  Nor let thy bawling fellows rack their throats,
    Nor the cropped herbage shoot another head.       5
      But when the fields are still,
  And the tired men and dogs all gone to rest,
    And only the white sheep are sometimes seen
    Cross and recross the strips of moon-blanched green;
  Come, Shepherd, and again renew the quest.       10

Here, where the reaper was at work of late,
  In this high field's dark corner, where he leaves
    His coat, his basket, and his earthen cruise,
  And in the sun all morning binds the sheaves,
    Then here, at noon, comes back his stores to use;       15
      Here will I sit and wait,
  While to my ear from uplands far away
    The bleating of the folded flocks is borne;
    With distant cries of reapers in the corn –
  All the live murmur of a summer's day.       20

Screened is this nook o'er the high, half-reaped field,
  And here till sun-down, Shepherd, will I be.
    Through the thick corn the scarlet poppies peep
  And round green roots and yellowing stalks I see
    Pale pink convolvulus in tendrils creep:       25
      And air-swept lindens yield
  Their scent, and rustle down their perfumed showers
    Of bloom on the bent grass where I am laid,
    And bower me from the August sun with shade;
  And the eye travels down to Oxford's towers.       30

And near me on the grass lies Glanvil's book –
  Come, let me read the oft-read tale again,
    The story of the Oxford scholar poor
  Of pregnant parts and quick inventive brain,
    Who, tired of knocking at Preferment's door,       35
      One summer morn forsook
  His friends, and went to learn the Gipsy lore,
    And roamed the world with that wild brotherhood,
    And came, as most men deemed, to little good,
  But came to Oxford and his friends no more.       40

But once, years after, in the country lanes
  Two scholars, whom at college erst he knew
    Met him, and of his way of life enquired.
  Whereat he answered, that the Gipsy crew,
    His mates, had arts to rule as they desired       45

The workings of men's brains;
And they can bind them to what thoughts they will:
'And I,' he said, 'the secret of their art,
When fully learned, will to the world impart:
But it needs happy moments for this skill.'                    50

This said, he left them, and returned no more.
But rumours hung about the countryside,
That the lost Scholar long was seen to stray,
Seen by rare glimpses, pensive and tongue-tied,
In hat of antique shape, and cloak of grey,                    55
The same the Gipsies wore.
Shepherds had met him on the Hurst in spring;
At some lone alehouse in the Berkshire moors,
On the warm ingle bench, the smock-frocked boors
Had found him seated at their entering,                        60

But, mid their drink and clatter, he would fly:
And I myself seem half to know thy looks,
And put the shepherds, Wanderer, on thy trace;
And boys who in lone wheatfields scare the rooks
I ask if thou hast passed their quiet place;                   65
Or in my boat I lie
Moored to the cool bank in the summer heats,
Mid wide grass meadows which the sunshine fills,
And watch the warm green muffled Cumnor hills,
And wonder if thou haunt'st their shy retreats.                70

For most, I know, thou lov'st retired ground.
Thee, at the ferry, Oxford riders blithe,
Returning home on summer nights, have met
Crossing the stripling Thames at Bablock-hithe,
Trailing in the cool stream thy fingers wet,                   75
As the slow punt swings round:
And leaning backward in a pensive dream,
And fostering in thy lap a heap of flowers
Plucked in shy fields and distant woodland bowers,
And thine eyes resting on the moonlit stream                   80

And then they land, and thou art seen no more.
Maidens, who from the distant hamlets come
To dance around the Fyfield elm in May,
Oft through the darkening fields have seen thee roam,
Or cross a stile into the public way.                          85
Oft thou hast given them store
Of flowers – the frail-leafed, white anemone –
Dark bluebells drenched with dews of summer eves –
And purple orchises with spotted leaves –
But none hath words she can report of thee.                    90

And, above Godstow Bridge, when haytime's here
  In June, and many a scythe in sunshine flames,
    Men who through those wide fields of breezy grass
    Where black-winged swallows haunt the glittering Thames,
      To bathe in the abandoned lasher pass,        95
        Have often passed thee near
  Sitting upon the river bank o'ergrown:
    Marked thy outlandish garb, thy figure spare,
    Thy dark vague eyes, and soft abstracted air;
But, when they came from bathing, thou wert gone.     100

At some lone homestead in the Cumnor hills,
  Where at her open door the housewife darns,
    Thou hast been seen, or hanging on a gate
  To watch the threshers in the mossy barns.
      Children, who early range these slopes and late     105
        For cresses from the rills,
  Have known thee watching, all an April day,
    The springing pastures and the feeding kine;
    And marked thee, when the stars come out and shine,
Through the long dewy grass move slow away.     110

In Autumn, on the skirts of Bagley Wood
  Where most the Gipsies by the turf-edged way
    Pitch their smoked tents, and every bush you see
  With scarlet patches tagged and shreds of grey,
      Above the forest ground called Thessaly –     115
        The blackbird picking food
  Sees thee, nor stops his meal, nor fears at all;
    So often has he known thee past him stray
    Rapt, twirling in thy hand a withered spray,
And waiting for the spark from Heaven to fall.     120

And once, in winter, on the causeway chill
  Where home through flooded fields foot-travellers go,
    Have I not passed thee on the wooden bridge,
  Wrapt in thy cloak and battling with the snow,
      Thy face towards Hinksey and its wintry ridge?     125
        And thou hast climbed the hill,
  And gained the white brow of the Cumnor range,
    Turned once to watch, while thick the snowflakes fall,
    The line of festal light in Christ-Church hall –
Then sought thy straw in some sequestered grange.     130

But what – I dream! Two hundred years are flown
  Since first thy story ran through Oxford halls,
    And the grave Glanvil did the tale inscribe
    That thou wert wandered from the studious walls

To learn strange arts, and join a Gipsy tribe:                    135
    And thou from earth art gone
Long since, and in some quiet churchyard laid;
    Some country nook, where o'er thy unknown grave
    Tall grasses and white flowering nettles wave,
Under a dark, red-fruited yew-tree's shade.                       140


– No, no, thou hast not felt the lapse of hours.
    For what wears out the life of mortal men?
        'Tis that from change to change their being rolls:
    'Tis that repeated shocks, again, again,
        Exhaust the energy of strongest souls,                    145
            And numb the elastic powers.
    Till having used our nerves with bliss and teen,
        And tired upon a thousand schemes our wit,
        To the just-pausing Genius we remit
    Our worn-out life, and are – what we have been.              150


Thou hast not lived, why should'st thou perish, so?
    Thou hadst *one* aim, *one* business, *one* desire:
        Else wert thou long since numbered with the dead –
    Else hadst thou spent, like other men, thy fire.
        The generations of thy peers are fled,                   155
            And we ourselves shall go;
    But thou possessest an immortal lot,
        And we imagine thee exempt from age
        And living as thou liv'st on Glanvil's page,
    Because thou hadst – what we, alas, have not.                160


For early didst thou leave the world, with powers
    Fresh, undiverted to the world without,
        Firm to their mark, not spent on other things;
    Free from the sick fatigue, the languid doubt,
        Which much to have tried, in much been baffled, brings.  165
            O life unlike to ours!
    Who fluctuate idly without term or scope,
        Of whom each strives, nor knows for what he strives,
        And each half lives a hundred different lives;
    Who wait like thee, but not, like thee, in hope.             170


Thou waitest for the spark from Heaven and we,
    Light half-believers of our casual creeds,
        Who never deeply felt, nor clearly willed,
    Whose insight never has borne fruit in deeds,
        Whose vague resolves never have been fulfilled;          175
            For whom each year we see
    Breeds new beginnings, disappointments new;
        Who hesitate and falter life away,

And lose tomorrow the ground won today –
Ah! do not we, Wanderer, await it too?                           180

Yes, we await it, but it still delays,
  And then we suffer and amongst us One,
    Who most has suffered, takes dejectedly
  His seat upon the intellectual throne;
    And all his store of sad experience he          185
      Lays bare of wretched days;
  Tells us his misery's birth and growth and signs,
    And how the dying spark of hope was fed,
    And how the breast was soothed, and how the head,
  And all his hourly varied anodynes.                           190

This for our wisest: and we others pine,
  And wish the long unhappy dream would end,
    And waive all claim to bliss, and try to bear
  With close-lipped Patience for our only friend,
    Sad Patience, too near neighbour to Despair:          195
      But none has hope like thine.
  Thou through the fields and through the woods dost stray,
    Roaming the country side, a truant boy,
    Nursing thy project in unclouded joy,
  And every doubt long blown by time away.                      200

O born in days when wits were fresh and clear,
  And life ran gaily as the sparkling Thames;
    Before this strange disease of modern life,
  With its sick hurry, its divided aims,
    Its heads o'ertaxed, its palsied hearts, was rife –          205
      Fly hence, our contact fear!
  Still fly, plunge deeper in the bowering wood!
    Averse, as Dido did with gesture stern
    From her false friend's approach in Hades turn,
  Wave us away, and keep thy solitude!                          210

Still nursing the unconquerable hope,
  Still clutching the inviolable shade,
    With a free onward impulse brushing through,
  By night, the silvered branches of the glade –
    Far on the forest skirts, where none pursue,          215
      On some mild pastoral slope
  Emerge, and resting on the moonlit pales,
    Freshen thy flowers, as in former years,
    With dew, or listen with enchanted ears,
  From the dark dingles, to the nightingales.                   220

But fly our paths, our feverish contact fly!
  For strong the infection of our mental strife,
    Which, though it gives no bliss, yet spoils for rest;
  And we should win thee from thy own fair life,
    Like us distracted, and like us unblest.           225
      Soon, soon thy cheer would die,
  Thy hopes grow timorous, and unfixed thy powers,
    And thy clear aims be cross and shifting made:
    And then thy glad perennial youth would fade,
  Fade, and grow old at last and die like ours.       230

Then fly our greetings, fly our speech and smiles!
  – As some grave Tyrian trader, from the sea,
    Descried at sunrise an emerging prow
  Lifting the cool-haired creepers stealthily,
    The fringes of a southward-facing brow             235
      Among the Ægean isles;
  And saw the merry Grecian coaster come,
    Freighted with amber grapes, and Chian wine,
    Green bursting figs, and tunnies steeped in brine;
  And knew the intruders on his ancient home,         240

The young light-hearted Masters of the waves;
  And snatched his rudder, and shook out more sail,
    And day and night held on indignantly
  O'er the blue Midland waters with the gale,
    Betwixt the Syrtes and soft Sicily,                245
      To where the Atlantic raves
  Outside the Western Straits, and unbent sails
    There, where down cloudy cliffs, through sheets of foam,
    Shy traffickers, the dark Iberians come;
  And on the beach undid his corded bales.            250

# Dante Gabriel Rossetti (1828–1882)

## The Blessed Damozel

The blessed Damozel leaned out
  From the gold bar of Heaven:
Her blue grave eyes were deeper much
  Than a deep water, even.
She had three lilies in her hand,             5
  And the stars in her hair were seven.

Her robe, ungirt from clasp to hem,
  No wrought flowers did adorn,
But a white rose of Mary's gift
  On the neck meetly worn;             10
And her hair, lying down her back,
  Was yellow like ripe corn.

Her seemed she scarce had been a day
  One of God's choristers;
The wonder was not yet quite gone        15
  From that still look of hers;
Albeit to them she left, her day
  Had counted as ten years.

(To *one* it is ten years of years:
  . . . . . . . Yet now, here in this place     20
Surely she leaned o'er me, – her hair
  Fell all about my face . . . . . . .
Nothing: the Autumn-fall of leaves.
  The whole year sets apace.)

It was the terrace of God's house         25
  That she was standing on, –
By God built over the sheer depth
  In which Space is begun;
So high, that looking downward thence,
  She could scarce see the sun.         30

It lies from Heaven across the flood
  Of ether, as a bridge.

Beneath, the tides of day and night
  With flame and blackness ridge
The void, as low as where this earth                    35
  Spins like a fretful midge.

But in those tracts, with her, it was
  The peace of utter light
And silence. For no breeze may stir
  Along the steady flight                               40
Of seraphim; no echo there,
  Beyond all depth or height.

Heard hardly, some of her new friends,
  Playing at holy games,
Spake, gentle-mouthed, among themselves,                45
  Their virginal chaste names;
And the souls, mounting up to God,
  Went by her like thin flames.

And still she bowed herself, and stooped
  Into the vast waste calm;                             50
Till her bosom's pressure must have made
  The bar she leaned on warm,
And the lilies lay as if asleep
  Along her bended arm.

From the fixt lull of heaven, she saw                   55
  Time, like a pulse, shake fierce
Through all the worlds. Her gaze still strove,
  In that steep gulph, to pierce
The swarm: and then she spake, as when
  The stars sang in their spheres.                      60

'I wish that he were come to me,
  For he will come,' she said.
'Have I not prayed in solemn heaven?
  On earth, has he not prayed?
Are not two prayers a perfect strength?                 65
  And shall I feel afraid?

'When round his head the aureole clings,
  And he is clothed in white,
I'll take his hand, and go with him
  To the deep wells of light,                           70
And we will step down as to a stream
  And bathe there in God's sight.

'We two will stand beside that shrine,
  Occult, withheld, untrod,

Whose lamps tremble continually 75
   With prayer sent up to God;
And where each need, revealed, expects
   Its patient period.

'We two will lie i' the shadow of
   That living mystic tree 80
Within whose secret growth the Dove
   Sometimes is felt to be,
While every leaf that His plumes touch
   Saith His name audibly.

'And I myself, will teach to him – 85
   I myself, lying so, –
The songs I sing here; which his mouth
   Shall pause in, hushed and slow,
Finding some knowledge at each pause
   And some new thing to know.' 90

(Alas! to *her* wise simple mind
   These things were all but known
Before: they trembled on her sense, –
   Her voice had caught their tone.
Alas for lonely Heaven! Alas 95
   For life wrung out alone!

Alas, and though the end were reached? . . .
   Was *thy* part understood
Or borne in trust? And for her sake
   Shall this too be found good? – 100
May the close lips that knew not prayer
   Praise ever, though they would?)

'We two,' she said, 'will seek the groves
   Where the lady Mary is,
With her five handmaidens, whose names 105
   Are five sweet symphonies: –
Cecily, Gertrude, Magdalen,
   Margaret, and Rosalys.

'Circle-wise sit they, with bound locks
   And bosoms covered;
Into the fine cloth, white like flame, 110
   Weaving the golden thread,
To fashion the birth-robes for them
   Who are just born, being dead.

'He shall fear haply, and be dumb. 115
   Then I will lay my cheek

To his, and tell about our love,
  Not once abashed or weak:
And the dear Mother will approve
  My pride, and let me speak.                          120

'Herself shall bring us, hand in hand,
  To Him round whom all souls
Kneel – the unnumbered solemn heads
  Bowed with their aureoles:
And Angels, meeting us, shall sing                     125
  To their citherns and citoles.

'There will I ask of Christ the Lord
  Thus much for him and me: –
To have more blessing than on earth
  In nowise; but to be                                 130
As then we were, – being as then
  At peace. Yea, verily.

'Yea, verily; when he is come
  We will do thus and thus:
Till this my vigil seem quite strange                  135
  And almost fabulous;
We two will live at once, one life;
  And peace shall be with us.'

She gazed, and listened, and then said,
  Less sad of speech than mild:                        140
  'All this is when he comes.' She ceased;
  The light thrilled past her, filled
With Angels, in strong level lapse.
  Her eyes prayed, and she smiled.

(I saw her smile.) But soon their flight               145
  Was vague 'mid the poised spheres.
And then she cast her arms along
  The golden barriers,
And laid her face between her hands,
  And wept. (I heard her tears.)                       150

## FROM: THE HOUSE OF LIFE: A SONNET-SEQUENCE

### Part I Youth and Change
### Sonnet VI: The Kiss

What smouldering senses in death's sick delay
  Or seizure of malign vicissitude

Can rob this body of honour, or denude
This soul of wedding-raiment worn today?
For lo! even now my lady's lips did play                                    5
   With these my lips such consonant interlude
   As laurelled Orpheus longed for when he wooed
The half-drawn hungering face with that last lay.

I was a child beneath her touch, – a man
   When breast to breast we clung, even I and she, –         10
   A spirit when her spirit looked through me, –
A god when all our life-breath met to fan
Our life-blood, till love's emulous ardours ran,
   Fire within fire, desire in deity.

## Sonnet VII: Supreme Surrender

To all the spirits of Love that wander by
   Along his love-sown harvest-field of sleep
   My lady lies apparent; and the deep
Calls to the deep; and no man sees but I.
The bliss so long afar, at length so nigh,                                    5
   Rests there attained. Methinks proud Love must weep
   When Fate's control doth from his harvest reap
The sacred hour for which the years did sigh.

First touched, the hand now warm around my neck
   Taught memory long to mock desire: and lo!                  10
   Across my breast the abandoned hair doth flow,
Where one shorn tress long stirred the longing ache:
And next the heart that trembled for its sake
   Lies the queen-heart in sovereign overthrow.

## Sonnet XI: The Love-Letter

Warmed by her hand and shadowed by her hair
   As close she leaned and poured her heart through thee,
   Whereof the articulate throbs accompany
The smooth black stream that makes thy whiteness fair, –
Sweet fluttering sheet, even of her breath aware, –                           5
   Oh let thy silent song disclose to me
   That soul wherewith her lips and eyes agree
Like married music in Love's answering air.

Fain had I watched her when, at some fond thought,
   Her bosom to the writing closelier pressed,                  10
   And her breast's secrets peered into her breast;

When, through eyes raised an instant, her soul sought
My soul, and from the sudden confluence caught
   The words that made her love the loveliest.


## Sonnet XXVI: Mid-Rapture

Thou lovely and beloved, thou my love;
   Whose kiss seems still the first; whose summoning eyes,
   Even now, as for our love-world's new sunrise,
Shed very dawn; whose voice, attuned above
All modulation of the deep-bowered dove,          5
   Is like a hand laid softly on the soul;
   Whose hand is like a sweet voice to control
Those worn tired brows it hath the keeping of: –

What word can answer to thy word, – what gaze
   To thine, which now absorbs within its sphere        10
   My worshipping face, till I am mirrored there
Light-circled in a heaven of deep-drawn rays?
What clasp, what kiss mine inmost heart can prove,
   O lovely and beloved, O my love?


## Sonnet LIII: Without Her

What of her glass without her? The blank grey
   There where the pool is blind of the moon's face.
   Her dress without her? The tossed empty space
Of cloud-rack whence the moon has passed away.
Her paths without her? Day's appointed sway        5
   Usurped by desolate night. Her pillowed place
   Without her? Tears, ah me! for love's good grace,
And cold forgetfulness of night or day.

What of the heart without her? Nay, poor heart,
   Of thee what word remains ere speech be still?        10
   A wayfarer by barren ways and chill,
Steep ways and weary, without her thou art,
Where the long cloud, the long wood's counterpart,
   Sheds doubled darkness up the labouring hill.


## Sonnet LIV: Love's Fatality

Sweet Love, – but oh! most dread Desire of Love
   Life-thwarted. Linked in gyves I saw them stand,
   Love shackled with vain-longing, hand to hand:

And one was eyed as the blue vault above:
But hope tempestuous like a fire-cloud hove     5
   I' the other's gaze, even as in his whose wand
   Vainly all night with spell-wrought power has spanned
The unyielding caves of some deep treasure-trove.

Also his lips, two writhen flakes of flame,
   Made moan: 'Alas O love, thus leashed with me!     10
   Wing-footed thou, wing-shouldered, once born free:
And I, thy cowering self, in chains grown tame, –
Bound to thy body and soul, named with thy name, –
   Life's iron heart, even Love's Fatality.'

# Part II: Change and Fate

## Sonnet LXIX: Autumn Idleness

This sunlight shames November where he grieves
   In dead red leaves, and will not let him shun
   The day, though bough with bough be overrun.
But with a blessing every glade receives
High salutation; while from hillock-eaves     5
   The deer gaze calling, dappled white and dun,
   As if, being foresters of old, the sun
Had marked them with the shade of forest-leaves.

Here dawn today unveiled her magic glass;
   Here noon now gives the thirst and takes the dew;     10
   Till eve bring rest when other good things pass.
And here the lost hours the lost hours renew
While I still lead my shadow o'er the grass,
   Nor know, for longing, that which I should do.

## Sonnet LXXVII: Soul's Beauty

Under the arch of Life, where love and death,
   Terror and mystery, guard her shrine, I saw
   Beauty enthroned; and though her gaze struck awe,
I drew it in as simply as my breath.
Hers are the eyes which, over and beneath,     5
   The sky and sea bend on thee, – which can draw,
   By sea or sky or woman, to one law,
The alloted bondman of her palm and wreath.

This is that Lady Beauty, in whose praise
   Thy voice and hand shake still, – long known to thee     10

By flying hair and fluttering hem, – the beat
  Following her daily of thy heart and feet,
  How passionately and irretrievably,
In what fond flight, how many ways and days!

## Sonnet LXXVIII: Body's Beauty

Of Adam's first wife, Lilith, it is told
  (The witch he loved before the gift of Eve,)
  That, ere the snake's, her sweet tongue could deceive,
And her enchanted hair was the first gold.
And still she sits, young while the earth is old,     5
  And, subtly of herself contemplative,
  Draws men to watch the bright web she can weave,
Till heart and body and life are in its hold.

The rose and poppy are her flowers; for where
  Is he not found, O Lilith, whom shed scent     10
And soft-shed kisses and soft sleep shall snare?
  Lo! as that youth's eyes burned at thine, so went
  Thy spell through him, and left his straight neck bent
And round his heart one strangling golden hair.

## Sonnet LXXXI: Memorial Thresholds

What place so strange, – though unrevealèd snow
  With unimaginable fires arise
  At the earth's end, – what passion of surprise
Like frost-bound fire-girt scenes of long ago?
Lo! this is none but I this hour; and lo!     5
  This is the very place which to mine eyes
  Those mortal hours in vain immortalize,
'Mid hurrying crowds, with what alone I know.

City, of thine a single simple door,
  By some new Power reduplicate, must be     10
  Even yet my life-porch in eternity,
Even with one presence filled, as once of yore:
Or mocking winds whirl round a chaff-strown floor
  Thee and thy years and these my words and me.

## Sonnet LXXXII: Hoarded Joy

I said: 'Nay, pluck not, – let the first fruit be:
  Even as thou sayest, it is sweet and red,

But let it ripen still. The tree's bent head
Sees in the stream its own fecundity
And bides the day of fulness. Shall not we             5
   At the sun's hour that day possess the shade,
   And claim our fruit before its ripeness fade,
And eat it from the branch and praise the tree?'

I say: 'Alas! our fruit hath wooed the sun
   Too long, – 'tis fallen and floats adown the stream.    10
Lo, the last clusters! Pluck them every one,
   And let us sup with summer; ere the gleam
Of autumn set the year's pent sorrow free,
And the woods wail like echoes from the sea.'

## Sonnet XCVII: A Superscription

Look in my face; my name is Might-have-been;
   I am also called No-more, Too-late, Farewell;
   Unto thine ear I hold the dead-sea shell
Cast up thy Life's foam-fretted feet between;
Unto thine eyes the glass where that is seen        5
   Which had Life's form and Love's, but by my spell
   Is now a shaken shadow intolerable,
Of ultimate things unuttered the frail screen.

Mark me, how still I am! But should there dart
   One moment through thy soul the soft surprise    10
   Of that winged Peace which lulls the breath of sighs, –
Then shalt thou see me smile, and turn apart
Thy visage to mine ambush at thy heart
   Sleepless with cold commemorative eyes.

## Sonnet CI: The One Hope

When vain desire at last and vain regret
   Go hand in hand to death, and all is vain,
   What shall assuage the unforgotten pain
And teach the unforgetful to forget?
Shall Peace be still a sunk stream long unmet, –    5
   Or may the soul at once in a green plain
   Stoop through the spray of some sweet life-fountain
And cull the dew-drenched flowering amulet?

Ah! when the wan soul in that golden air
   Between the scriptured petals softly blown    10
   Peers breathless for the gift of grace unknown, –

Ah! let none other alien spell soe'er
But only the one Hope's one name be there, –
  Not less nor more, but even that word alone.


## Nuptial Sleep

At length their long kiss severed, with sweet smart:
  And as the last slow sudden drops are shed
  From sparkling eaves when all the storm has fled,
So singly flagged the pulses of each heart.
Their bosoms sundered, with the opening start                 5
  Of married flowers to either side outspread
  From the knit stem; yet still their mouths, burnt red,
Fawned on each other where they lay apart.

Sleep sank them lower than the tide of dreams,
  And their dreams watched them sink, and slid away.          10
Slowly their souls swam up again, through gleams
  Of watered light and dull drowned waifs of day;
Till from some wonder of new woods and streams
  He woke, and wondered more: for there she lay.


## 'Found'

### *(For a Picture)*

'There is a budding morrow in midnight:' –
  So sang our Keats, our English nightingale.
  And here, as lamps across the bridge turn pale
In London's smokeless resurrection-light,
Dark breaks to dawn. But o'er the deadly blight              5
  Of Love deflowered and sorrow of none avail
  Which makes this man gasp and this woman quail,
Can day from darkness ever again take flight?

Ah! gave not these two hearts their mutual pledge,
Under one mantle sheltered 'neath the hedge                  10
  In gloaming courtship? And, O God! today
He only knows he holds her; – but what part
Can life now take? She cries in her locked heart, –
  'Leave me – I do not know you – go away!'

# Christina G. Rossetti
# (1830–1894)

## Remember

Remember me when I am gone away,
    Gone far away into the silent land;
    When you can no more hold me by the hand,
Nor I half turn to go yet turning stay.
Remember me when no more day by day         5
    You tell me of our future that you planned:
    Only remember me; you understand
It will be late to counsel then or pray.
Yet if you should forget me for a while
    And afterwards remember, do not grieve:         10
    For if the darkness and corruption leave
    A vestige of the thoughts that once I had,
Better by far you should forget and smile
Than that you should remember and be sad.

## Goblin Market

Morning and evening
Maids heard the goblins cry:
'Come buy our orchard fruits,
Come buy, come buy:
Apples and quinces,         5
Lemons and oranges,
Plump unpecked cherries,
Melons and raspberries,
Bloom-down-cheeked peaches,
Swart-headed mulberries,         10
Wild free-born cranberries,
Crab-apples, dewberries,
Pine-apples, blackberries,
Apricots, strawberries; –
All ripe together         15
In summer weather, –
Morns that pass by,
Fair eves that fly;

Come buy, come buy:
Our grapes fresh from the vine,                                    20
Pomegranates full and fine,
Dates and sharp bullaces,
Rare pears and greengages,
Damsons and bilberries,
Taste them and try:                                                25
Currants and gooseberries,
Bright-fire-like barberries,
Figs to fill your mouth,
Citrons from the South,
Sweet to tongue and sound to eye;                                  30
Come buy, come buy.'

   Evening by evening
Among the brookside rushes,
Laura bowed her head to hear,
Lizzie veiled her blushes:                                         35
Crouching close together
In the cooling weather,
With clasping arms and cautioning lips,
With tingling cheeks and finger tips.
'Lie close,' Laura said,                                           40
Pricking up her golden head:
'We must not look at goblin men,
We must not buy their fruits:
Who knows upon what soil they fed
Their hungry thirsty roots?'                                       45
'Come buy,' call the goblins
Hobbling down the glen.
'Oh,' cried Lizzie, 'Laura, Laura,
You should not peep at goblin men.'
Lizzie covered up her eyes,                                        50
Covered close lest they should look;
Laura reared her glossy head,
And whispered like the restless brook:
'Look, Lizzie, look, Lizzie,
Down the glen tramp little men.                                    55
One hauls a basket,
One bears a plate,
One lugs a golden dish
Of many pounds weight.
How fair the vine must grow                                        60
Whose grapes are so luscious;
How warm the wind must blow
Through those fruit bushes.'
'No,' said Lizzie: 'No, no, no;
Their offers should not charm us,                                  65

Their evil gifts would harm us.'
She thrust a dimpled finger
In each ear, shut eyes and ran:
Curious Laura chose to linger
Wondering at each merchant man.                              70
One had a cat's face,
One whisked a tail,
One tramped at a rat's pace,
One crawled like a snail,
One like a wombat prowled obtuse and furry,                  75
One like a ratel tumbled hurry skurry.
She heard a voice like voice of doves
Cooing all together:
They sounded kind and full of loves
In the pleasant weather.                                     80

   Laura stretched her gleaming neck
Like a rush-imbedded swan,
Like a lily from the beck,
Like a moonlit poplar branch,
Like a vessel at the launch                                  85
When its last restraint is gone.

   Backwards up the mossy glen
Turned and trooped the goblin men,
With their shrill repeated cry,
'Come buy, come buy.'                                        90
When they reached where Laura was
They stood stock still upon the moss,
Leering at each other,
Brother with queer brother;
Signalling each other,                                       95
Brother with sly brother.
One set his basket down,
One reared his plate;
One began to weave a crown
Of tendrils, leaves, and rough nuts brown                   100
(Men sell not such in any town);
One heaved the golden weight
Of dish and fruit to offer her:
'Come buy, come buy,' was still their cry.
Laura stared but did not stir,                               105
Longed but had no money:
The whisk-tailed merchant bade her taste
In tones as smooth as honey,
The cat-faced purred,
The rat-paced spoke a word                                   110
Of welcome, and the snail-paced even was heard;

One parrot-voiced and jolly
Cried 'Pretty Goblin' still for 'Pretty Polly;' –
One whistled like a bird.

    But sweet-tooth Laura spoke in haste:          115
'Good folk, I have no coin;
To take were to purloin:
I have no copper in my purse,
I have no silver either,
And all my gold is on the furze          120
That shakes in windy weather
Above the rusty heather.'
'You have much gold upon your head,'
They answered all together:
'Buy from us with a golden curl.'          125
She clipped a precious golden lock,
She dropped a tear more rare than pearl,
Then sucked their fruit globes fair or red:
Sweeter than honey from the rock,
Stronger than man-rejoicing wine,          130
Clearer than water flowed that juice;
She never tasted such before,
How should it cloy with length of use?
She sucked and sucked and sucked the more
Fruits which that unknown orchard bore;         135
She sucked until her lips were sore;
Then flung the emptied rinds away
But gathered up one kernel-stone,
And knew not was it night or day
As she turned home alone.          140

    Lizzie met her at the gate
Full of wise upbraidings:
'Dear, you should not stay so late,
Twilight is not good for maidens;
Should not loiter in the glen          145
In the haunts of goblin men.
Do you not remember Jeanie,
How she met them in the moonlight,
Took their gifts both choice and many,
Ate their fruits and wore their flowers         150
Plucked from bowers
Where summer ripens at all hours?
But ever in the moonlight
She pined and pined away;
Sought them by night and day,         155
Found them no more but dwindled and grew grey;
Then fell with the first snow,

While to this day no grass will grow
Where she lies low:
I planted daisies there a year ago                    160
That never blow.
You should not loiter so.'
'Nay, hush,' said Laura:
'Nay, hush, my sister:
I ate and ate my fill,                                165
Yet my mouth waters still;
To-morrow night I will
Buy more:' and kissed her:
'Have done with sorrow;
I'll bring you plums to-morrow                         170
Fresh on their mother twigs,
Cherries worth getting;
You cannot think what figs
My teeth have met in,
What melons icy-cold                                   175
Piled on a dish of gold
Too huge for me to hold,
What peaches with a velvet nap,
Pellucid grapes without one seed:
Odorous indeed must be the mead                       180
Whereon they grow, and pure the wave they drink
With lilies at the brink,
And sugar-sweet their sap.'

  Golden head by golden head,
Like two pigeons in one nest                          185
Folded in each other's wings,
They lay down in their curtained bed:
Like two blossoms on one stem,
Like two flakes of new-fallen snow,
Like two wands of ivory                               190
Tipped with gold for awful kings.
Moon and stars gazed in at them,
Wind sang to them lullaby,
Lumbering owls forbore to fly,
Not a bat flapped to and fro                          195
Round their nest:
Cheek to cheek and breast to breast
Locked together in one nest.

  Early in the morning
When the first cock crowed his warning,               200
Neat like bees, as sweet and busy,
Laura rose with Lizzie:
Fetched in honey, milked the cows,

Aired and set to rights the house,
Kneaded cakes of whitest wheat,                                    205
Cakes for dainty mouths to eat,
Next churned butter, whipped up cream,
Fed their poultry, sat and sewed;
Talked as modest maidens should:
Lizzie with an open heart,                                        210
Laura in an absent dream,
One content, one sick in part;
One warbling for the mere bright day's delight,
One longing for the night.

　　At length slow evening came:                                  215
They went with pitchers to the reedy brook;
Lizzie most placid in her look,
Laura most like a leaping flame.
They drew the gurgling water from its deep;
Lizzie plucked purple and rich golden flags,                      220
Then turning homewards said: 'The sunset flushes
Those furthest loftiest crags;
Come, Laura, not another maiden lags,
No wilful squirrel wags,
The beasts and birds are fast asleep.'                            225
But Laura loitered still among the rushes
And said the bank was steep.

　　And said the hour was early still,
The dew not fallen, the wind not chill:
Listening ever, but not catching                                  230
The customary cry,
'Come buy, come buy,'
With its iterated jingle
Of sugar-baited words:
Not for all her watching                                          235
Once discerning even one goblin
Racing, whisking, tumbling, hobbling;
Let alone the herds
That used to tramp along the glen,
In groups or single,                                              240
Of brisk fruit-merchant men.

　　Till Lizzie urged, 'O Laura, come;
I hear the fruit-call but I dare not look:
You should not loiter longer at this brook:
Come with me home.                                                245
The stars rise, the moon bends her arc,
Each glowworm winks her spark,
Let us get home before the night grows dark:

For clouds may gather
Though this is summer weather,                                    250
Put out the lights and drench us through;
Then if we lost our way what should we do?'

   Laura turned cold as stone
To find her sister heard that cry alone,
That goblin cry,                                                 255
'Come buy our fruits, come buy.'
Must she then buy no more such dainty fruits?
Must she no more such succous pasture find,
Gone deaf and blind?
Her tree of life drooped from the root:                          260
She said not one word in her heart's sore ache;
But peering thro' the dimness, nought discerning,
Trudged home, her pitcher dripping all the way;
So crept to bed, and lay
Silent till Lizzie slept;                                        265
Then sat up in a passionate yearning,
And gnashed her teeth for baulked desire, and wept
As if her heart would break.

   Day after day, night after night,
Laura kept watch in vain                                         270
In sullen silence of exceeding pain.
She never caught again the goblin cry:
'Come buy, come buy;' –
She never spied the goblin men
Hawking their fruits along the glen:                             275
But when the noon waxed bright
Her hair grew thin and grey;
She dwindled, as the fair full moon doth turn
To swift decay and burn
Her fire away.                                                   280

   One day remembering her kernel-stone
She set it by a wall that faced the south;
Dewed it with tears, hoped for a root,
Watched for a waxing shoot,
But there came none;                                            285
It never saw the sun,
It never felt the trickling moisture run:
While with sunk eyes and faded mouth
She dreamed of melons, as a traveller sees
False waves in desert drouth                                     290
With shade of leaf-crowned trees,
And burns the thirstier in the sandful breeze.

She no more swept the house,
Tended the fowls or cows,
Fetched honey, kneaded cakes of wheat,                    295
Brought water from the brook:
But sat down listless in the chimney-nook
And would not eat.

Tender Lizzie could not bear
To watch her sister's cankerous care                     300
Yet not to share.
She night and morning
Caught the goblins' cry:
'Come buy our orchard fruits,
Come buy, come buy:' –                                    305
Beside the brook, along the glen,
She heard the tramp of goblin men,
The voice and stir
Poor Laura could not hear;
Longed to buy fruit to comfort her,                      310
But feared to pay too dear.
She thought of Jeanie in her grave,
Who should have been a bride;
But who for joys brides hope to have
Fell sick and died                                       315
In her gay prime,
In earliest Winter time,
With the first glazing rime,
With the first snowfall of crisp Winter time.

Till Laura dwindling                                     320
Seemed knocking at Death's door:
Then Lizzie weighed no more
Better and worse;
But put a silver penny in her purse,
Kissed Laura, crossed the heath with clumps of furze     325
At twilight, halted by the brook:
And for the first time in her life
Began to listen and look.

Laughed every goblin
When they spied her peeping:                              330
Came towards her hobbling,
Flying, running, leaping,
Puffing and blowing,
Chuckling, clapping, crowing,
Clucking and gobbling,                                    335
Mopping and mowing,
Full of airs and graces,

Pulling wry faces,
Demure grimaces,
Cat-like and rat-like,                                     340
Ratel- and wombat-like,
Snail-paced in a hurry,
Parrot-voiced and whistler,
Helter skelter, hurry skurry,
Chattering like magpies,                                  345
Fluttering like pigeons,
Gliding like fishes, –
Hugged her and kissed her:
Squeezed and caressed her:
Stretched up their dishes,                                350
Panniers, and plates:
'Look at our apples
Russet and dun,
Bob at our cherries,
Bite at our peaches,                                      355
Citrons and dates,
Grapes for the asking,
Pears red with basking
Out in the sun,
Plums on their twigs;                                     360
Pluck them and suck them,
Pomegranates, figs.' –

'Good folk,' said Lizzie,
Mindful of Jeanie:
'Give me much and many:' –                                365
Held out her apron,
Tossed them her penny.
'Nay, take a seat with us,
Honour and eat with us,'
They answered grinning:                                   370
'Our feast is but beginning.
Night yet is early,
Warm and dew-pearly,
Wakeful and starry:
Such fruits as these                                      375
No man can carry;
Half their bloom would fly,
Half their dew would dry,
Half their flavour would pass by.
Sit down and feast with us,                               380
Be welcome guest with us,
Cheer you and rest with us.' –
'Thank you,' said Lizzie: 'But one waits
At home alone for me:

So without further parleying,                                385
If you will not sell me any
Of your fruits though much and many,
Give me back my silver penny
I tossed you for a fee.' –
They began to scratch their pates,                           390
No longer wagging, purring,
But visibly demurring,
Grunting and snarling.
One called her proud,
Cross-grained, uncivil;                                      395
Their tones waxed loud,
Their looks were evil.
Lashing their tails
They trod and hustled her,
Elbowed and jostled her,                                     400
Clawed with their nails,
Barking, mewing, hissing, mocking,
Tore her gown and soiled her stocking,
Twitched her hair out by the roots,
Stamped upon her tender feet,                                405
Held her hands and squeezed their fruits
Against her mouth to make her eat.

   White and golden Lizzie stood,
Like a lily in a flood, –
Like a rock of blue-veined stone                             410
Lashed by tides obstreperously, –
Like a beacon left alone
In a hoary roaring sea,
Sending up a golden fire, –
Like a fruit-crowned orange-tree                             415
White with blossoms honey-sweet
Sore beset by wasp and bee, –
Like a royal virgin town
Topped with gilded dome and spire
Close beleaguered by a fleet                                 420
Mad to tug her standard down.

   One may lead a horse to water,
Twenty cannot make him drink.
Though the goblins cuffed and caught her,
Coaxed and fought her,                                       425
Bullied and besought her,
Scratched her, pinched her black as ink,
Kicked and knocked her,
Mauled and mocked her,
Lizzie uttered not a word;                                   430

Would not open lip from lip
Lest they should cram a mouthful in:
But laughed in heart to feel the drip
Of juice that syrupped all her face,
And lodged in dimples of her chin,                          435
And streaked her neck which quaked like curd.
At last the evil people
Worn out by her resistance
Flung back her penny, kicked their fruit
Along whichever road they took,                             440
Not leaving root or stone or shoot;
Some writhed into the ground,
Some dived into the brook
With ring and ripple,
Some scudded on the gale without a sound,                   445
Some vanished in the distance.

   In a smart, ache, tingle,
Lizzie went her way;
Knew not was it night or day;
Sprang up the bank, tore thro' the furze,                   450
Threaded copse and dingle,
And heard her penny jingle
Bouncing in her purse, –
Its bounce was music to her ear.
She ran and ran                                             455
As if she feared some goblin man
Dogged her with gibe or curse
Or something worse:
But not one goblin skurried after,
Nor was she pricked by fear;                                460
The kind heart made her windy-paced
That urged her home quite out of breath with haste
And inward laughter.

   She cried 'Laura,' up the garden,
'Did you miss me?                                           465
Come and kiss me.
Never mind my bruises,
Hug me, kiss me, suck my juices
Squeezed from goblin fruits for you,
Goblin pulp and goblin dew.                                 470
Eat me, drink me, love me;
Laura, make much of me:
For your sake I have braved the glen
And had to do with goblin merchant men.'

   Laura started from her chair,                            475
Flung her arms up in the air,

Clutched her hair:
'Lizzie, Lizzie, have you tasted
For my sake the fruit forbidden?
Must your light like mine be hidden,                         480
Your young life like mine be wasted,
Undone in mine undoing
And ruined in my ruin,
Thirsty, cankered, goblin-ridden?' –
She clung about her sister,                                  485
Kissed and kissed and kissed her:
Tears once again
Refreshed her shrunken eyes,
Dropping like rain
After long sultry drouth;                                    490
Shaking with aguish fear, and pain,
She kissed and kissed her with a hungry mouth.

  Her lips began to scorch,
That juice was wormwood to her tongue,
She loathed the feast:                                       495
Writhing as one possessed she leaped and sung,
Rent all her robe, and wrung
Her hands in lamentable haste,
And beat her breast.
Her locks streamed like the torch                            500
Borne by a racer at full speed,
Or like the mane of horses in their flight,
Or like an eagle when she stems the light
Straight toward the sun,
Or like a caged thing freed,                                 505
Or like a flying flag when armies run.

  Swift fire spread through her veins, knocked at her heart,
Met the fire smouldering there
And overbore its lesser flame;
She gorged on bitterness without a name;                     510
Ah! fool, to choose such part
Of soul-consuming care!
Sense failed in the mortal strife:
Like the watch-tower of a town
Which an earthquake shatters down,                           515
Like a lightning-stricken mast,
Like a wind-uprooted tree
Spun about,
Like a foam-topped waterspout
Cast down headlong in the sea,                               520
She fell at last;

Pleasure past and anguish past,
Is it death or is it life?

  Life out of death.
That night long Lizzie watched by her,                           525
Counted her pulse's flagging stir,
Felt for her breath,
Held water to her lips, and cooled her face
With tears and fanning leaves:
But when the first birds chirped about their eaves,              530
And early reapers plodded to the place
Of golden sheaves,
And dew-wet grass
Bowed in the morning winds so brisk to pass,
And new buds with new day                                        535
Opened of cup-like lilies on the stream,
Laura awoke as from a dream,
Laughed in the innocent old way,
Hugged Lizzie but not twice or thrice;
Her gleaming locks showed not one thread of grey,               540
Her breath was sweet as May
And light danced in her eyes.

  Days, weeks, months, years
Afterwards, when both were wives
With children of their own;                                      545
Their mother-hearts beset with fears,
Their lives bound up in tender lives;
Laura would call the little ones
And tell them of her early prime,
Those pleasant days long gone                                    550
Of not-returning time:
Would talk about the haunted glen,
The wicked, quaint fruit-merchant men,
Their fruits like honey to the throat
But poison in the blood                                          555
(Men sell not such in any town);
Would tell them how her sister stood
In deadly peril to do her good,
And win the fiery antidote:
Then joining hands to little hands                               560
Would bid them cling together,
'For there is no friend like a sister
In calm or stormy weather;
To cheer one on the tedious way,
To fetch one if one goes astray,                                 565
To lift one if one totters down,
To strengthen whilst one stands.'

# *Thomas Hardy (1840–1928)*

## Neutral Tones

We stood by a pond that winter day,
And the sun was white, as though chidden of God,
And a few leaves lay on the starving sod,
  – They had fallen from an ash, and were gray.

Your eyes on me were as eyes that rove                     5
Over tedious riddles of years ago;
And some words played between us to and fro –
  On which lost the more by our love.

The smile on your mouth was the deadest thing
Alive enough to have strength to die;                      10
And a grin of bitterness swept thereby
  Like an ominous bird a-wing. . . .

Since then, keen lessons that love deceives,
And wrings with wrong, have shaped to me
Your face, and the God-curst sun, and a tree,             15
  And a pond edged with grayish leaves.


## Nature's Questioning

When I look forth at dawning, pool,
      Field, flock, and lonely tree,
      All seem to gaze at me
Like chastened children sitting silent in a school;

      Their faces dulled, constrained, and worn,          5
          As though the master's way
          Through the long teaching day
Had cowed them till their early zest was overborne.

      Upon them stirs in lippings mere
          (As if once clear in call,                       10
          But now scarce breathed at all)—
'We wonder, ever wonder, why we find us here!

'Has some Vast Imbecility,
 Mighty to build and blend,
  But impotent to tend,
Framed us in jest, and left us now to hazardry?     15

'Or come we of an Automaton
 Unconscious of our pains? . . .
  Or are we live remains
Of Godhead dying downwards, brain and eye now gone?   20

'Or is it that some high Plan betides,
 As yet not understood,
  Of Evil stormed by Good,
We the Forlorn Hope over which Achievement strides?'

Thus things around. No answerer I. . . .       25
 Meanwhile the winds, and rains,
  And Earth's old glooms and pains
Are still the same, and Life and Death are neighbours nigh.

# The Impercipient

## *(At a Cathedral Service)*

That with this bright believing band
 I have no claim to be,
That faiths by which my comrades stand
 Seem fantasies to me,
And mirage-mists their Shining Land,       5
 Is a strange destiny.

Why thus my soul should be consigned
 To infelicity,
Why always I must feel as blind
 To sights my brethren see,        10
Why joys they have found I cannot find,
 Abides a mystery.

Since heart of mine knows not that ease
 Which they know; since it be
That He who breathes All's Well to these     15
 Breathes no All's-Well to me,
My lack might move their sympathies
 And Christian charity!

I am like a gazer who should mark
 An inland company         20

Standing upfingered, with, 'Hark! hark!
    The glorious distant sea!'
And feel, 'Alas, 'tis but yon dark
    And wind-swept pine to me!'

Yet I would bear my shortcomings         25
    With meet tranquillity,
But for the charge that blessed things
    I'd liefer not have be.
O, doth a bird beshorn of wings
    Go earth-bound wilfully!         30

    . . . . . . . .

Enough. As yet disquiet clings
    About us. Rest shall we.


# In a Eweleaze near Weatherbury

The years have gathered grayly
    Since I danced upon this leaze
With one who kindled gaily
    Love's fitful ecstasies!
But despite the term as teacher,         5
    I remain what I was then
In each essential feature
    Of the fantasies of men.

Yet I note the little chisel
    Of never-napping Time         10
Defacing wan and grizzel
    The blazon of my prime.
When at night he thinks me sleeping
    I feel him boring sly
Within my bones, and heaping         15
    Quaintest pains for by-and-by.

Still, I'd go the world with Beauty,
    I would laugh with her and sing,
I would shun divinest duty
    To resume her worshipping.         20
But she'd scorn my brave endeavour,
    She would not balm the breeze
By murmuring 'Thine for ever!'
    As she did upon this leaze.

        1890.

## 'I look into my glass'

I look into my glass,
And view my wasting skin,
And say, 'Would God it came to pass
My heart had shrunk as thin!'

For then, I, undistrest                                                    5
By hearts grown cold to me,
Could lonely wait my endless rest
With equanimity.

But Time, to make me grieve,
Part steals, lets part abide;                                          10
And shakes this fragile frame at eve
With throbbings of noontide.

## A Broken Appointment

You did not come,
And marching Time drew on, and wore me numb.—
Yet less for loss of your dear presence there
Than that I thus found lacking in your make
That high compassion which can overbear          5
Reluctance for pure lovingkindness' sake
Grieved I, when, as the hope-hour stroked its sum,
You did not come.

You love not me,
And love alone can lend you loyalty;                      10
—I know and knew it. But, unto the store
Of human deeds divine in all but name,
Was it not worth a little hour or more
To add yet this: Once you, a woman, came
To soothe a time-torn man; even though it be
You love not me?                                                      15

## The Darkling Thrush

I leant upon a coppice gate
When Frost was spectre-gray,
And Winter's dregs made desolate
The weakening eye of day.
The tangled bine-stems scored the sky               5
Like strings of broken lyres,

And all mankind that haunted nigh
  Had sought their household fires.

The land's sharp features seemed to be
  The Century's corpse outleant,    10
His crypt the cloudy canopy,
  The wind his death-lament.
The ancient pulse of germ and birth
  Was shrunken hard and dry,
And every spirit upon earth     15
  Seemed fervourless as I.

At once a voice arose among
  The bleak twigs overhead
In a full-hearted evensong
  Of joy illimited;     20
An aged thrush, frail, gaunt, and small,
  In blast-beruffled plume,
Had chosen thus to fling his soul
  Upon the growing gloom.

So little cause for carolings    25
  Of such ecstatic sound
Was written on terrestrial things
  Afar or nigh around,
That I could think there trembled through
  His happy goodnight air    30
Some blessed Hope, whereof he knew
  And I was unaware.
       31st December 1900

# The Self-Unseeing

Here is the ancient floor,
Footworn and hollowed and thin,
Here was the former door
Where the dead feet walked in.

She sat here in her chair,     5
Smiling into the fire;
He who played stood there,
Bowing it higher and higher.

Childlike, I danced in a dream;
Blessings emblazoned that day;   10
Everything glowed with a gleam;
Yet we were looking away!

# Gerard Manley Hopkins (1844–1889)

## The Wreck of the Deutschland

*To the*
*happy memory of five Franciscan nuns*
*exiles by the Falck Laws*
*drowned between midnight and morning of*
*Dec. 7th, 1875*

*Part the First*

### 1

Thou mastering me
God! giver of breath and bread;
World's strand, sway of the sea;
Lord of living and dead;
Thou hast bound bones and veins in me, fastened me flesh,                5
And after it almost unmade, what with dread,
Thy doing: and dost thou touch me afresh?
Over again I feel thy finger and find thee.

### 2

I did say yes
O at lightning and lashed rod;                                            10
Thou heardst me truer than tongue confess
Thy terror, O Christ, O God;
Thou knowest the walls, altar and hour and night:
The swoon of a heart that the sweep and the hurl of thee trod
Hard down with a horror of height:                                        15
And the midriff astrain with leaning of, laced with fire of stress.

### 3

The frown of his face
Before me, the hurtle of hell
Behind, where, where was a, where was a place?
I whirled out wings that spell                                            20
And fled with a fling of the heart to the heart of the Host.
My heart, but you were dovewinged, I can tell,

Carrier-witted, I am bold to boast,
To flash from the flame to the flame then, tower from the grace to the grace.

4

I am soft sift                                                                    25
   In an hourglass – at the wall
Fast, but mined with a motion, a drift,
   And it crowds and it combs to the fall;
I steady as a water in a well, to a poise, to a pane,
   But roped with, always, all the way down from the tall                         30
      Fells or flanks of the voel, a vein
Of the gospel proffer, a pressure, a principle, Christ's gift.

5

I kiss my hand
   To the stars, lovely-asunder
Starlight, wafting him out of it; and                                             35
   Glow, glory in thunder;
Kiss my hand to the dappled-with-damson west:
   Since, tho' he is under the world's splendour and wonder,
      His mystery must be instressed, stressed;
For I greet him the days I meet him, and bless when I understand.                 40

6

Not out of his bliss
   Springs the stress felt
Nor first from heaven (and few know this)
   Swings the stroke dealt –
Stroke and a stress that stars and storms deliver,                               45
That guilt is hushed by, hearts are flushed by and melt –
   But it rides time like riding a river
(And here the faithful waver, the faithless fable and miss).

7

It dates from day
   Of his going in Galilee;                                                       50
Warm-laid grave of a womb-life grey;
   Manger, maiden's knee;
The dense and the driven Passion, and frightful sweat:
Thence the discharge of it, there its swelling to be,
   Though felt before, though in high flood yet –                                 55
What none would have known of it, only the heart, being hard at bay,

8

Is out with it! Oh,
   We lash with the best or worst
Word last! How a lush-kept plush-capped sloe

   Will, mouthed to flesh-burst,          60
  Gush! – flush the man, the being with it, sour or sweet,
 Brim, in a flash, full! – Hither then, last or first,
   To hero of Calvary, Christ's feet –
Never ask if meaning it, wanting it, warned of it – men go.

9

   Be adored among men,           65
   God, three-numberèd form;
  Wring thy rebel, dogged in den,
   Man's malice, with wrecking and storm.
 Beyond saying sweet, past telling of tongue,
 Thou art lightning and love, I found it, a winter and warm;   70
  Father and fondler of heart thou hast wrung:
Hast thy dark descending and most art merciful then.

10

   With an anvil-ding
   And with fire in him forge thy will
  Or rather, rather then, stealing as Spring      75
   Through him, melt him but master him still:
 Whether at once, as once at a crash Paul,
 Or as Austin, a lingering-out swéet skíll,
  Make mercy in all of us, out of us all
Mastery, but be adored, but be adored King.       80

*Part the Second*

11

  'Some find me a sword; some
   The flange and the rail; flame,
  Fang, or flood' goes Death on drum,
   And storms bugle his fame.
 But wé dream we are rooted in earth – Dust!      85
 Flesh falls within sight of us, we, though our flower the same,
  Wave with the meadow, forget that there must
The sour scythe cringe, and the blear share come.

12

  On Saturday sailed from Bremen,
   American-outward-bound,          90
  Take settler and seamen, tell men with women,
   Two hundred souls in the round –
 O Father, not under thy feathers nor ever as guessing
 The goal was a shoal, of a fourth the doom to be drowned;
  Yet did the dark side of the bay of thy blessing    95
Not vault them, the million of rounds of thy mercy not reeve even them in?

### 13

Into the snows she sweeps,
　　Hurling the haven behind,
　The Deutschland, on Sunday; and so the sky keeps,
　　For the infinite air is unkind,                                    100
And the sea flint-flake, black-backed in the regular blow,
Sitting Eastnortheast, in cursed quarter, the wind;
　　Wiry and white-fiery and whirlwind-swivellèd snow
Spins to the widow-making unchilding unfathering deeps.

### 14

She drove in the dark to leeward,                                     105
　　She struck – not a reef or a rock
　But the combs of a smother of sand: night drew her
　　Dead to the Kentish Knock;
And she beat the bank down with her bows and the ride of her keel;
The breakers rolled on her beam with ruinous shock;                   110
　　And canvas and compass, the whorl and the wheel
Idle for ever to waft her or wind her with, these she endured.

### 15

Hope had grown grey hairs,
　　Hope had mourning on,
　Trenched with tears, carved with cares,                             115
　　Hope was twelve hours gone;
And frightful a nightfall folded rueful a day
Nor rescue, only rocket and lightship, shone,
　　And lives at last were washing away:
To the shrouds they took, – they shook in the hurling and horrible airs.   120

### 16

One stirred from the rigging to save
　　The wild woman-kind below,
　With a rope's end round the man, handy and brave –
　　He was pitched to his death at a blow,
For all his dreadnought breast and braids of thew:                    125
They could tell him for hours, dandled the to and fro
　　Through the cobbled foam-fleece. What could he do
With the burl of the fountains of air, buck and the flood of the wave?

### 17

They fought with God's cold –
　　And they could not and fell to the deck                           130
　(Crushed them) or water (and drowned them) or rolled
　　With the sea-romp over the wreck.
Night roared, with the heart-break hearing a heart-broke rabble,
The woman's wailing, the crying of child without check –

Till a lioness arose breasting the babble, 135
A prophetess towered in the tumult, a virginal tongue told.

18

Ah, touched in your bower of bone,
Are you! turned for an exquisite smart,
Have you! make words break from me here all alone,
Do you! – mother of being in me, heart. 140
O unteachably after evil, but uttering truth,
Why, tears! is it? tears; such a melting, a madrigal start!
Never-eldering revel and river of youth,
What can it be, this glee? the good you have there of your own?

19

Sister, a sister calling 145
A master, her master and mine! –
And the inboard seas run swirling and hawling;
The rash smart sloggering brine
Blinds her; but she that weather sees one thing, one;
Has one fetch in her: she rears herself to divine 150
Ears, and the call of the tall nun
To the men in the tops and the tackle rode over the storm's brawling.

20

She was first of a five and came
Of a coifèd sisterhood.
(O Deutschland, double a desperate name! 155
O world wide of its good!
But Gertrude, lily, and Luther, are two of a town,
Christ's lily and beast of the waste wood:
From life's dawn it is drawn down,
Abel is Cain's brother and breasts they have sucked the same.) 160

21

Loathed for a love men knew in them,
Banned by the land of their birth,
Rhine refused them, Thames would ruin them;
Surf, snow, river and earth
Gnashed: but thou art above, thou Orion of light; 165
Thy unchancelling poising palms were weighing the worth,
Thou martyr-master: in thy sight
Storm flakes were scroll-leaved flowers, lily showers – sweet heaven was
astrew in them.

22

Five! the finding and sake
And cipher of suffering Christ. 170
Mark, the mark is of man's make

And the word of it Sacrificed.
But he scores it in scarlet himself on his own bespoken,
Before-time-taken, dearest prizèd and priced –
    Stigma, signal, cinquefoil token                                    175
For lettering of the lamb's fleece, ruddying of the rose-flake.


### 23

Joy fall to thee, father Francis,
    Drawn to the Life that died;
With the gnarls of the nails in thee, niche of the lance, his
    Lovescape crucified                                                180
And seal of his seraph-arrival! and these thy daughters
And five-livèd and leavèd favour and pride,
    Are sisterly sealed in wild waters,
To bathe in his fall-gold mercies, to breathe in his all-fire glances.


### 24

Away in the loveable west,                                             185
    On a pastoral forehead of Wales,
I was under a roof here, I was at rest,
    And they the prey of the gales;
She to the black-about air, to the breaker, the thickly
Falling flakes, to the throng that catches and quails                  190
    Was calling 'O Christ, Christ, come quickly':
The cross to her she calls Christ to her, christens her wild-worst Best.


### 25

The majesty! what did she mean?
    Breathe, arch and original Breath.
Is it love in her of the being as her lover had been?                  195
    Breathe, body of lovely Death.
They were else-minded then, altogether, the men
Woke thee with a *We are perishing* in the weather of Gennesareth.
    Or is it that she cried for the crown then,
The keener to come at the comfort for feeling the combating keen?      200


### 26

For how to the heart's cheering
    The down-dugged ground-hugged grey
Hovers off, the jay-blue heavens appearing
    Of pied and peeled May!
Blue-beating and hoary-glow height; or night, still higher,           205
With belled fire and the moth-soft Milky Way,
    What by your measure is the heaven of desire,
The treasure never eyesight got, nor was ever guessed what for the hearing?


### 27

No, but it was not these.
    The jading and jar of the cart,                                    210

Time's tasking, it is fathers that asking for ease
    Of the sodden-with-its-sorrowing heart,
Not danger, electrical horror; then further it finds
    The appealing of the Passion is tenderer in prayer apart:
        Other, I gather, in measure her mind's        215
Burden, in wind's burly and beat of endragonèd seas.

### 28

But how shall I ... make me room there:
    Reach me a ` ... Fancy, come faster –
Strike you the sight of it? look at it loom there,
    Thing that she ... There then! the Master,        220
*Ipse*, the only one, Christ, King, Head:
    He was to cure the extremity where he had cast her;
        Do, deal, lord it with living and dead;
Let him ride, her pride, in his triumph, despatch and have done with his
    doom there.

### 29

Ah! there was a heart right!        225
    There was single eye!
Read the unshapeable shock night
    And knew the who and the why;
Wording it how but by him that present and past,
Heaven and earth are word of, worded by? –        230
    The Simon Peter of a soul! to the blast
Tarpeïan-fast, but a blown beacon of light.

### 30

Jesu, heart's light,
    Jesu, maid's son,
What was the feast followed the night        235
    Thou hadst glory of this nun? –
Feast of the one woman without stain.
    For so conceivèd, so to conceive thee is done;
        But here was heart-throe, birth of a brain,
Word, that heard and kept thee and uttered thee outright.        240

### 31

Well, she has thee for the pain, for the
    Patience; but pity of the rest of them!
Heart, go and bleed at a bitterer vein for the
    Comfortless unconfessed of them –
No not uncomforted: lovely-felicitous Providence        245
Finger of a tender of, O of a feathery delicacy, the breast of the
    Maiden could obey so, be a bell to, ring of it, and
Startle the poor sheep back! is the shipwrack then a harvest, does tempest
    carry the grain for thee?

### 32

    I admire thee, master of the tides,
      Of the Yore-flood, of the year's fall;           250
    The recurb and the recovery of the gulf's sides,
      The girth of it and the wharf of it and the wall;
  Stanching, quenching ocean of a motionable mind;
  Ground of being, and granite of it: past all
    Grasp God, throned behind           255
Death with a sovereignty that heeds but hides, bodes but abides;

### 33

    With a mercy that outrides
      The all of water, an ark
    For the listener; for the lingerer with a love glides
      Lower than death and the dark;          260
  A vein for the visiting of the past-prayer, pent in prison,
  The-last-breath penitent spirits – the uttermost mark
    Our passion-plungèd giant risen,
The Christ of the Father compassionate, fetched in the storm of his strides.

### 34

    Now burn, new born to the world,          265
      Double-naturèd name,
    The heaven-flung, heart-fleshed, maiden-furled
      Miracle-in-Mary-of-flame,
  Mid-numberèd he in three of the thunder-throne!
  Not a dooms-day dazzle in his coming nor dark as he came;     270
    Kind, but royally reclaiming his own;
A released shower, let flash to the shire, not a lightning of fire hard-hurled.

### 35

    Dame, at our door
      Drowned, and among our shoals,
    Remember us in the roads, the heaven-haven of the reward:     275
      Our King back, Oh, upon English souls!
  Let him easter in us, be a dayspring to the dimness of us, be a
      crimson-cresseted east,
  More brightening her, rare-dear Britain, as his reign rolls,
    Pride, rose, prince, hero of us, high-priest,
Our hearts' charity's hearth's fire, our thoughts' chivalry's throng's Lord.     280

# God's Grandeur

The world is charged with the grandeur of God.
    It will flame out, like shining from shook foil;

It gathers to a greatness, like the ooze of oil
Crushed. Why do men then now not reck his rod?
Generations have trod, have trod, have trod;                    5
    And all is seared with trade; bleared, smeared with toil;
    And wears man's smudge and shares man's smell: the soil
Is bare now, nor can foot feel, being shod.

And for all this, nature is never spent;
    There lives the dearest freshness deep down things;          10
And though the last lights off the black West went
    Oh, morning, at the brown brink eastward, springs –
Because the Holy Ghost over the bent
    World broods with warm breast and with ah! bright wings.

# The Windhover

*To Christ our Lord*

I caught this morning morning's minion, king-
    dom of daylight's dauphin, dapple-dawn-drawn Falcon, in his riding
    Of the rolling level underneath him steady air, and striding
High there, how he rung upon the rein of a wimpling wing
In his ecstasy! then off, off forth on swing,                   5
    As a skate's heel sweeps smooth on a bow-bend: the hurl and gliding
    Rebuffed the big wind. My heart in hiding
Stirred for a bird, – the achieve of, the mastery of the thing!

Brute beauty and valour and act, oh, air, pride, plume, here
    Buckle! AND the fire that breaks from thee then, a billion    10
Times told lovelier, more dangerous, O my chevalier!

    No wonder of it: shéer plód makes plough down sillion
Shine, and blue-bleak embers, ah my dear,
    Fall, gall themselves, and gash gold-vermilion.

# Pied Beauty

Glory be to God for dappled things –
    For skies of couple-colour as a brinded cow;
        For rose-moles all in stipple upon trout that swim;
Fresh-firecoal chestnut-falls; finches' wings;
    Landscape plotted and pieced – fold, fallow, and plough;     5
        And áll trádes, their gear and tackle and trim.

All things counter, original, spare, strange;
    Whatever is fickle, freckled (who knows how?)

With swift, slow; sweet, sour; adazzle, dim;
He fathers-forth whose beauty is past change:          10
                                        Praise him.


# Binsey Poplars

### *Felled 1879*


My aspens dear, whose airy cages quelled,
     Quelled or quenched in leaves the leaping sun,
All felled, felled, are all felled;
   Of a fresh and following folded rank
          Not spared, not one                               5
            That dandled a sandalled
          Shadow that swam or sank
On meadow and river and wind-wandering weed-winding bank.

O if we but knew what we do
     When we delve or hew –                                10
   Hack and rack the growing green!
      Since country is so tender
   To touch, her being só slender,
   That, like this sleek and seeing ball
   But a prick will make no eye at all,                   15
   Where we, even where we mean
          To mend her we end her,
      When we hew or delve:
After-comers cannot guess the beauty been.
   Ten or twelve, only ten or twelve                      20
      Strokes of havoc únselve
          The sweet especial scene,
      Rural scene, a rural scene,
      Sweet especial rural scene.


# Felix Randal

Felix Randal the farrier, O is he dead then? my duty all ended,
Who have watched his mould of man, big-boned and hardy-handsome
Pining, pining, till time when reason rambled in it and some
Fatal four disorders, fleshed there, all contended?


Sickness broke him. Impatient, he cursed at first, but mended     5
Being anointed and all; though a heavenlier heart began some
Months earlier, since I had our sweet reprieve and ransom
Tendered to him. Ah well, God rest him all road ever he offended!

This seeing the sick endears them to us, us too it endears.
My tongue had taught thee comfort, touch had quenched thy tears,          10
Thy tears that touched my heart, child, Felix, poor Felix Randal;

How far from then forethought of, all thy more boisterous years,
When thou at the random grim forge, powerful amidst peers,
Didst fettle for the great grey drayhorse his bright and battering sandal!

## 'As Kingfishers Catch Fire'

As kingfishers catch fire, dragonflies draw flame;
   As tumbled over rim in roundy wells
   Stones ring; like each tucked string tells, each hung bell's
Bow swung finds tongue to fling out broad its name;          5
Each mortal thing does one thing and the same:
   Deals out that being indoors each one dwells;
   Selves – goes itself; *myself* it speaks and spells,
Crying *What I do is me: for that I came.*

Í say more: the just man justices;          10
   Keeps gráce: thát keeps all his goings graces;
Acts in God's eye what in God's eye he is –
   Chríst. For Christ plays in ten thousand places,
Lovely in limbs, and lovely in eyes not his
   To the Father through the features of men's faces.

## Spelt from Sibyl's Leaves

Earnest, earthless, equal, attuneable, | vaulty, voluminous, . . . stupendous
Evening strains to be tíme's vást, | womb-of-all, home-of-all, hearse-of-all night.
Her fond yellow hornlight wound to the west, | her wild hollow hoarlight hung
   to the height
Waste; her earliest stars, earlstars, | stárs principal, overbend us,
Fíre-féaturing heaven. For earth | her being has unbound; her dapple is at
   end, as-          5
tray or aswarm, all through her, in throngs; | self ín self steepèd and páshed
   – qúite
Disremembering, dísmémbering | áll now. Heart, you round me right
With: Óur évening is over us; óur night | whélms, whélms, ánd will end us.

Only the beakleaved boughs dragonish | damask the tool-smooth bleak light;
   black,
Ever so black on it. Óur tale, O óur oracle! | Lét life, wáned, ah lét life wind          10
Off hér once skéined stained véined varíety | upon, áll on twó spools; párt, pen,
   páck

Now her áll in twó flocks, twó folds – black, white; | right, wrong; reckon but, reck
 but, mind
But thése two; wáre of a wórld where bút these | twó tell, each off the óther;
 of a rack
Where, selfwrung, selfstrung, sheathe-and shelterless, | thóughts agaínst
 thoughts ín groans grínd.

## 'Thou art indeed just, Lord'

*Justus quidem tu es, Domine, si disputem tecum; verumtamen*
*justa loquar ad te: Quare via impiorum prosperatur? &c.*

Thou art indeed just, Lord, if I contend
With thee; but, sir, so what I plead is just.
Why do sinners' ways prosper? and why must
Disappointment all I endeavour end?

Wert thou my enemy, O thou my friend,      5
How wouldst thou worse, I wonder, than thou dost
Defeat, thwart me? Oh, the sots and thralls of lust
Do in spare hours more thrive than I that spend,

Sir, life upon thy cause. See, banks and brakes
Now, leavèd how thick! lacèd they are again     10
With fretty chervil, look, and fresh wind shakes

Them; birds build – but not I build; no, but strain,
Time's eunuch, and not breed one work that wakes.
Mine, O thou lord of life, send my roots rain.

# A. E. Housman
# (1859–1936)

## From: A Shropshire Lad

### I
### *1887*

From Clee to heaven the beacon burns,
   The shires have seen it plain,
From north and south the sign returns
   And beacons burn again.

Look left, look right, the hills are bright,          5
   The dales are light between,
Because 'tis fifty years tonight
   That God has saved the Queen.

Now, when the flame they watch not towers
   About the soil they trod,                10
Lads, we'll remember friends of ours
   Who shared the work with God.

To skies that knit their heartstrings right,
   To fields that bred them brave,
The saviours come not home to-night:        15
   Themselves they could not save.

It dawns in Asia, tombstones show
   And Shropshire names are read;
And the Nile spills his overflow
   Beside the Severn's dead.             20

We pledge in peace by farm and town
   The Queen they served in war,
And fire the beacons up and down
   The land they perished for.

'God save the Queen' we living sing,        25
   From height to height 'tis heard;
And with the rest your voices ring,
   Lads of the Fifty-third.

Oh, God will save her, fear you not:
  Be you the men you've been,                                    30
Get you the sons your fathers got,
  And God will save the Queen.


## II

Loveliest of trees, the cherry now
Is hung with bloom along the bough,
And stands about the woodland ride
Wearing white for Eastertide.

Now, of my threescore years and ten,                                   5
Twenty will not come again,
And take from seventy springs a score,
It only leaves me fifty more.

And since to look at things in bloom
Fifty springs are little room,                                         10
About the woodlands I will go
To see the cherry hung with snow.


## IV
### *Reveille*

Wake: the silver dusk returning
  Up the beach of darkness brims,
And the ship of sunrise burning
  Strands upon the eastern rims.

Wake: the vaulted shadow shatters,                                     5
  Trampled to the floor it spanned,
And the tent of night in tatters
  Straws the sky-pavilioned land.

Up, lad, up, 'tis late for lying:
  Hear the drums of morning play;                               10
Hark, the empty highways crying
  'Who'll beyond the hills away?'

Towns and countries woo together,
  Forelands beacon, belfries call;
Never lad that trod on leather                                         15
  Lived to feast his heart with all.

Up, lad: thews that lie and cumber
  Sunlit pallets never thrive;
Morns abed and daylight slumber
  Were not meant for man alive.                                  20

Clay lies still, but blood's a rover;
   Breath's a ware that will not keep.
Up, lad: when the journey's over
   There'll be time enough to sleep.

### XII

When I watch the living meet,
   And the moving pageant file
Warm and breathing through the street
   Where I lodge a little while,

If the heats of hate and lust 5
   In the house of flesh are strong,
Let me mind the house of dust
   Where my sojourn shall be long.

In the nation that is not
   Nothing stands that stood before; 10
There revenges are forgot,
   And the hater hates no more;

Lovers lying two and two
   Ask not whom they sleep beside,
And the bridegroom all night through 15
   Never turns him to the bride.

### XVI

It nods and curtseys and recovers
   When the wind blows above,
The nettle on the graves of lovers
   That hanged themselves for love.

The nettle nods, the wind blows over, 5
   The man, he does not move,
The lover of the grave, the lover
   That hanged himself for love.

### XIX
#### *To an Athlete Dying Young*

The time you won your town the race
We chaired you through the marketplace;
Man and boy stood cheering by,
And home we brought you shoulder-high.

Today, the road all runners come, 5
Shoulder-high we bring you home,
And set you at your threshold down,
Townsman of a stiller town.

Smart lad, to slip betimes away
From fields where glory does not stay                                    10
And early though the laurel grows
It withers quicker than the rose.

Eyes the shady night has shut
Cannot see the record cut,
And silence sounds no worse than cheers                                   15
After earth has stopped the ears:

Now you will not swell the rout
Of lads that wore their honours out,
Runners whom renown outran
And the name died before the man.                                        20

So set, before its echoes fade,
The fleet foot on the sill of shade,
And hold to the low lintel up
The still-defended challenge-cup.

XXVII

'Is my team ploughing,
    That I was used to drive
And hear the harness jingle
    When I was man alive?'

Ay, the horses trample,                                                  5
    The harness jingles now;
No change though you lie under
    The land you used to plough.

'Is football playing
    Along the river shore,                                               10
With lads to chase the leather,
    Now I stand up no more?'

Ay, the ball is flying,
    The lads play heart and soul;
The goal stands up, the keeper                                           15
    Stands up to keep the goal.

'Is my girl happy,
    That I thought hard to leave,
And has she tired of weeping
    As she lies down at eve?'                                            20

Ay, she lies down lightly,
    She lies not down to weep:

Your girl is well contented.
   Be still, my lad, and sleep.

'Is my friend hearty,                                25
   Now I am thin and pine,
And has he found to sleep in
   A better bed than mine?'

Yes, lad, I lie easy,
   I lie as lads would choose;                    30
I cheer a dead man's sweetheart,
   Never ask me whose.

XXX

Others, I am not the first,
Have willed more mischief than they durst:
If in the breathless night I too
Shiver now, 'tis nothing new.

More than I, if truth were told,                     5
Have stood and sweated hot and cold,
And through their reins in ice and fire
Fear contended with desire.

Agued once like me were they,
But I like them shall win my way                     10
Lastly to the bed of mould
Where there's neither heat nor cold.

But from my grave across my brow
Plays no wind of healing now,
And fire and ice within me fight .                   15
Beneath the suffocating night.

XXXI

On Wenlock Edge the wood's in trouble;
   His forest fleece the Wrekin heaves;
The gale, it plies the saplings double,
   And thick on Severn snow the leaves.

'Twould blow like this through holt and hanger       5
   When Uricon the city stood:
'Tis the old wind in the old anger,
   But then it threshed another wood.

Then, 'twas before my time, the Roman
   At yonder heaving hill would stare:            10
The blood that warms an English yeoman,
   The thoughts that hurt him, they were there.

There, like the wind through woods in riot,
  Through him the gale of life blew high;
The tree of man was never quiet:                    15
  Then 'twas the Roman, now 'tis I.

The gale, it plies the saplings double,
  It blows so hard, 'twill soon be gone:
Today the Roman and his trouble
  Are ashes under Uricon.                           20

### XL

Into my heart an air that kills
  From yon far country blows:
What are those blue remembered hills,
  What spires, what farms are those?

That is the land of lost content,                   5
  I see it shining plain,
The happy highways where I went
  And cannot come again.

### XLIV

Shot? so quick, so clean an ending?
  Oh that was right, lad, that was brave:
Yours was not an ill for mending,
  'Twas best to take it to the grave.

Oh you had forethought, you could reason,           5
  And saw your road and where it led,
And early wise and brave in season
  Put the pistol to your head.

Oh soon, and better so than later
  After long disgrace and scorn,                    10
You shot dead the household traitor,
  The soul that should not have been born.

Right you guessed the rising morrow
  And scorned to tread the mire you must:
Dust's your wages, son of sorrow,                   15
  But men may come to worse than dust.

Souls undone, undoing others, –
  Long time since the tale began.
You would not live to wrong your brothers:
  Oh lad, you died as fits a man.                   20

Now to your grave shall friend and stranger
  With ruth and some with envy come:

Undishonoured, clear of danger,
   Clean of guilt, pass hence and home.

Turn safe to rest, no dreams, no waking;                25
   And here, man, here's the wreath I've made:
'Tis not a gift that's worth the taking,
   But wear it and it will not fade.

## XLVI

   Bring, in this timeless grave to throw,
No cypress, sombre on the snow;
Snap not from the bitter yew
His leaves that live December through;
Break no rosemary, bright with rime                  5
And sparkling to the cruel clime;
Nor plod the winter land to look
For willows in the icy brook
To cast them leafless round him: bring
No spray that ever buds in spring.                  10

   But if the Christmas field has kept
Awns the last gleaner overstept,
Or shrivelled flax, whose flower is blue
A single season, never two;
Or if one haulm whose year is o'er                15
Shivers on the upland frore,
– Oh, bring from hill and stream and plain
Whatever will not flower again,
   To give him comfort: he and those
   Shall bide eternal bedfellows                20
   Where low upon the couch he lies
   Whence he never shall arise.

## XLVIII

Be still, my soul, be still; the arms you bear are brittle,
   Earth and high heaven are fixt of old and foundedstrong.
Think rather, – call to thought, if now you grieve a little,
   The days when we had rest, O soul, for they were long.

Men loved unkindness then, but lightless in the quarry      5
   I slept and saw not; tears fell down, I did not mourn;
Sweat ran and blood sprang out and I was never sorry:
   Then it was well with me, in days ere I was born.

Now, and I muse for why and never find the reason,
   I pace the earth, and drink the air, and feel the sun.      10
Be still, be still, my soul; it is but for a reason:
   Let us endure an hour and see injustice done.

Ay, look: high heaven and earth ail from the prime foundation;
    All thoughts to rive the heart are here, and all are vain:
Horror and scorn and hate and fear and indignation –        15
    Oh why did I awake? when shall I sleep again?

## LX

Now hollow fires burn out to black,
    And lights are guttering low:
Square your shoulders, lift your pack,
    And leave your friends and go.

Oh never fear, man, nought's to dread,        5
    Look not left nor right:
In all the endless road you tread
    There's nothing but the night.

## LXII

    'Terence, this is stupid stuff:
You eat your victuals fast enough;
There can't be much amiss, 'tis clear,
To see the rate you drink your beer.
But oh, good Lord, the verse you make,        5
It gives a chap the belly-ache.
The cow, the old cow, she is dead;
It sleeps well, the horned head:
We poor lads, 'tis our turn now
To hear such tunes as killed the cow.        10
Pretty friendship 'tis to rhyme
Your friends to death before their time
Moping melancholy mad:
Come, pipe a tune to dance to, lad.'

    Why, if 'tis dancing you would be,        15
There's brisker pipes than poetry.
Say, for what were hop-yards meant,
Or why was Burton built on Trent?
Oh many a peer of England brews
Livelier liquor than the Muse,        20
And malt does more than Milton can
To justify God's ways to man.
Ale, man, ale's the stuff to drink
For fellows whom it hurts to think:
Look into the pewter pot        25
To see the world as the world's not.
And faith, 'tis pleasant till 'tis past:
The mischief is that 'twill not last.
Oh I have been to Ludlow fair
And left my necktie God knows where,        30

And carried half way home, or near,
Pints and quarts of Ludlow beer:
Then the world seemed none so bad,
And I myself a sterling lad;
And down in lovely muck I've lain,           35
Happy till I woke again.
Then I saw the morning sky:
Heigho, the tale was all a lie;
The world, it was the old world yet,
I was I, my things were wet,           40
And nothing now remained to do
But begin the game anew.

   Therefore, since the world has still
Much good, but much less good than ill,
And while the sun and moon endure           45
Luck's a chance, but trouble's sure,
I'd face it as a wise man would,
And train for ill and not for good.
'Tis true, the stuff I bring for sale
Is not so brisk a brew as ale:           50
Out of a stem that scored the hand
I wrung it in a weary land.
But take it: if the smack is sour,
The better for the embittered hour;
It should do good to heart and head           55
When your soul is in my soul's stead;
And I will friend you, if I may,
In the dark and cloudy day.

   There was a king reigned in the East:
There, when kings will sit to feast,           60
They get their fill before they think
With poisoned meat and poisoned drink.
He gathered all that springs to birth
From the many-venomed earth;
First a little, thence to more,           65
He sampled all her killing store;
And easy, smiling, seasoned sound,
Sate the king when healths went round.
They put arsenic in his meat
And stared aghast to watch him eat;           70
They poured strychnine in his cup
And shook to see him drink it up:
They shook, they stared as white's their shirt:
Them it was their poison hurt.
– I tell the tale that I heard told.           75
Mithridates, he died old.

# From: *Last Poems*

## XL

Tell me not here, it needs not saying,
    What tune the enchantress plays
In aftermaths of soft September
    Or under blanching mays,
For she and I were long acquainted          5
    And I knew all her ways.

On russet floors, by waters idle,
    The pine lets fall its cone;
The cuckoo shouts all day at nothing
    In leafy dells alone;          10
And traveller's joy beguiles in autumn
    Hearts that have lost their own.

On acres of the seeded grasses
    The changing burnish heaves;
Or marshalled under moons of harvest         15
    Stand still all night the sheaves;
Or beeches strip in storms for winter
    And stain the wind with leaves.

Possess, as I possessed a season,
    The countries I resign,         20
Where over elmy plains the highway
    Would mount the hills and shine,
And full of shade the pillared forest
    Would murmur and be mine.

For nature, heartless, witless nature,         25
    Will neither care nor know
What stranger's feet may find the meadow
    And trespass there and go,
Nor ask amid the dews of morning
    If they are mine or no.         30

# William Butler Yeats
# (1865–1939)

## The Stolen Child

Where dips the rocky highland
Of Sleuth Wood in the lake
There lies a leafy island
Where flapping herons wake
The drowsy water-rats;                                           5
There we've hid our faery vats,
Full of berries
And of reddest stolen cherries.
And of reddest stolen cherries.
*Come away, O human child!*                                      10
*To the waters and the wild*
*With a faery, hand in hand,*
*For the world's more full of weeping than you can understand.*

Where the wave of moonlight glosses
The dim grey sands with light,                                   15
Far off by furthest Rosses
We foot it all the night,
Weaving olden dances,
Mingling hands and mingling glances
Till the moon has taken flight;                                  20
To and fro we leap
And chase the forthy bubbles,
While the world is full of troubles
And is anxious in its sleep.
*Come away, O human child!*                                      25
*To the waters and the wild*
*With a faery, hand in hand,*
*For the world's more full of weeping than you can understand.*

Where the wandering water gushes
From the hills above Glen-Car,                                   30
In pools among the rushes
That scarce could bathe a star,
We seek for slumbering trout
And whispering in their ears

Give them unquiet dreams;                                                    35
Leaning softly out
From ferns that drop their tears
Over the young streams.
*Come away, O human child!*
*To the waters and the wild*                                                  40
*With a faery, hand in hand,*
*For the world's more full of weeping than you can understand.*

Away with us he's going,
The solemn-eyed:
He'll hear no more the lowing                                                 45
Of the calves on the warm hillside
Or the kettle on the hob
Sing peace into his breast,
Or see the brown mice bob
Round and round the oatmeal-chest.                                           50
*For he comes, the human child,*
*To the waters and the wild*
*With a faery, hand in hand,*
*For the world's more full of weeping than he can understand.*

## Down by the Salley Gardens

Down by the salley gardens my love and I did meet;
She passed the salley gardens with little snow-white feet.
She bid me take love easy, as the leaves grow on the tree;
But I, being young and foolish, with her would not agree.

In a field by the river my love and I did stand,                             5
And on my leaning shoulder she laid her snow-white hand.
She bid me take life easy, as the grass grows on the weirs;
But I was young and foolish, and now am full of tears.

## The Rose of the World

Who dreamed that beauty passes like a dream?
For these red lips, with all their mournful pride,
Mournful that no new wonder may betide,
Troy passed away in one high funeral gleam,
And Usna's children died.                                                    5

We and the labouring world are passing by:
Amid men's souls, that waver and give place
Like the pale waters in their wintry race,
Under the passing stars, foam of the sky,
Lives on this lonely face.                                                   10

Bow down, archangels, in your dim abode:
Before you were, or any hearts to beat,
Weary and kind one lingered by His seat;
He made the world to be a grassy road
Before her wandering feet.                                    15

## The Lake Isle of Innisfree

I will arise and go now, and go to Innisfree,
And a small cabin build there, of clay and wattles made:
Nine bean rows will I have there, a hive for the honey bee,
And live alone in the bee-loud glade.

And I shall have some peace there, for peace comes dropping slow,     5
Dropping from the veils of the morning to where the cricket sings;
There midnight's all a glimmer, and noon a purple glow,
And evening full of the linnet's wings.

I will arise and go now, for always night and day
I hear lake water lapping with low sounds by the shore;          10
While I stand on the roadway, or on the pavements grey,
I hear it in the deep heart's core.

## When You Are Old

When you are old and grey and full of sleep,
And nodding by the fire, take down this book,
And slowly read, and dream of the soft look
Your eyes had once, and of their shadows deep;

How many loved your moments of glad grace,                       5
And loved your beauty with love false or true,
But one man loved the pilgrim soul in you,
And loved the sorrows of your changing face;

And bending down beside the glowing bars,
Murmur, a little sadly, how Love fled                            10
And paced upon the mountains overhead
And hid his face amid a crowd of stars.

## Who Goes with Fergus?

Who will go drive with Fergus now,
And pierce the deep wood's woven shade,
And dance upon the level shore?
Young man, lift up your russet brow,

And lift your tender eyelids, maid,                                          5
And brood on hopes and fear no more.

And no more turn aside and brood
Upon love's bitter mystery;
For Fergus rules the brazen cars,
And rules the shadows of the wood,                                          10
And the white breast of the dim sea
And all dishevelled wandering stars.


## The Lamentation of the Old Pensioner

Although I shelter from the rain
Under a broken tree,
My chair was nearest to the fire
In every company
That talked of love or politics,                                            5
Ere Time transfigured me.

Though lads are making pikes again
For some conspiracy,
And crazy rascals rage their fill
At human tyranny,                                                           10
My contemplations are of Time
That has transfigured me.

There's not a woman turns her face
Upon a broken tree,
And yet the beauties that I loved                                           15
Are in my memory;
I spit into the face of Time
That has transfigured me.


## The Song of Wandering Aengus

I went out to the hazel wood,
Because a fire was in my head,
And cut and peeled a hazel wand,
And hooked a berry to a thread;
And when white moths were on the wing,                                      5
And moth-like stars were flickering out,
I dropped the berry in a stream
And caught a little silver trout.

When I had laid it on the floor
I went to blow the fire aflame,                                             10
But something rustled on the floor,

And some one called me by my name:
It had become a glimmering girl
With apple blossom in her hair
Who called me by my name and ran                    15
And faded through the brightening air.

Though I am old with wandering
Through hollow lands and hilly lands,
I will find out where she has gone,
And kiss her lips and take her hands;               20
And walk among long dappled grass,
And pluck till time and times are done
The silver apples of the moon,
The golden apples of the sun.

## He Wishes for the Cloths of Heaven

Had I the heavens' embroidered cloths,
Enwrought with golden and silver light,
The blue and the dim and the dark cloths
Of night and light and the half light,
I would spread the cloths under your feet:          5
But I, being poor, have only my dreams;
I have spread my dreams under your feet;
Tread softly because you tread on my dreams.

## Adam's Curse

We sat together at one summer's end,
That beautiful mild woman, your close friend,
And you and I, and talked of poetry.
I said, 'A line will take us hours maybe;
Yet if it does not seem a moment's thought,         5
Our stitching and unstitching has been naught.

Better go down upon your marrow-bones
And scrub a kitchen pavement, or break stones
Like an old pauper, in all kinds of weather;
For to articulate sweet sounds together             10
Is to work harder than all these, and yet
Be thought an idler by the noisy set
Of bankers, schoolmasters, and clergymen
The martyrs call the world.'

                  And thereupon
That beautiful mild woman for whose sake            15

There's many a one shall find out all heartache
On finding that her voice is sweet and low
Replied, 'To be born woman is to know –
Although they do not talk of it at school –
That we must labour to be beautiful.'                          20

I said, 'It's certain there is no fine thing
Since Adam's fall but needs much labouring.
There have been lovers who thought love should be
So much compounded of high courtesy
That they would sigh and quote with learned looks            25
Precedents out of beautiful old books;
Yet now it seems an idle trade enough.'

We sat grown quiet at the name of love;
We saw the last embers of daylight die,
And in the trembling blue-green of the sky                    30
A moon, worn as if it had been a shell
Washed by time's waters as they rose and fell
About the stars and broke in days and years.

I had a thought for no one's but your ears:
That you were beautiful, and that I strove                    35
To love you in the old high way of love;
That it had all seemed happy, and yet we'd grown
As weary-hearted as that hollow moon.

# Red Hanrahan's Song about Ireland

The old brown thorn-trees break in two high over Cummen Strand,
Under a bitter black wind that blows from the left hand;
Our courage breaks like an old tree in a black wind and dies,
But we have hidden in our hearts the flame out of the eyes
Of Cathleen, the daughter of Houlihan.                        5

The wind has bundled up the clouds high over Knocknarea,
And thrown the thunder on the stones for all that Maeve can say.
Angers that are like noisy clouds have set our hearts abeat;
But we have all bent low and low and kissed the quiet feet
Of Cathleen, the daughter of Houlihan.                        10

The yellow pool has overflowed high up on Clooth-na-Bare,
For the wet winds are blowing out of the clinging air;
Like heavy flooded waters our bodies and our blood;
But purer than a tall candle before the Holy Rood
Is Cathleen, the daughter of Houlihan.                        15

# Index of Titles and First Lines